IMAGES
of America

ALONG THE
TOMS RIVER

BEACHWOOD, ISLAND HEIGHTS, OCEAN GATE,
PINE BEACH, SOUTH TOMS RIVER, TOMS RIVER

The history of Island Heights from 1878 to 1995 is spanned by the lives of the Reverend Simpson (1835–1913)and his grandson, H. Ormond Simpson (1908–1995). John Simpson became superintendent of the Island Heights Camp Meeting Association as soon as the land was purchased. He organized the Methodist Episcopal Church and was its first pastor; he also established the post office and became its first postmaster. When Island Heights became a borough in 1887, he was elected the first mayor. His grandson, H. Ormond Simpson, was the model for the Uncle Sam poster (1942) by Charles R. Chickering, and was an amateur artist active in the Ocean County Artists Guild.

IMAGES
of America

ALONG THE
TOMS RIVER

BEACHWOOD, ISLAND HEIGHTS, OCEAN GATE,
PINE BEACH, SOUTH TOMS RIVER, TOMS RIVER

Ocean County Historical Society
Publications Committee

Patricia H. Burke
Anne L. Camp
Robert H. Camp
Carolyn M. Campbell, Chair
Mary Ellen Hudson
William A. King Jr.
Jean C. Lacey
Estelle M. Martin
Elizabeth M. Morgan
Vilma R. Oxenford
Martha T. Smith
Thomas M. Williams

ARCADIA
PUBLISHING

Copyright © 2008 by Ocean County Historical Society
ISBN 978-1-5316-0875-0

Published by Arcadia Publishing
Charleston, South Carolina

Library of Congress Catalog Card Number: Applied for

For all general information contact Arcadia Publishing at:
Telephone 843-853-2070
Fax 843-853-0044
E-mail sales@arcadiapublishing.com
For customer service and orders:
Toll-Free 1-888-313-2665

Visit us on the Internet at www.arcadiapublishing.com

This is part of the Henley Avenue pier gang of Pine Beach, c. 1915, which enjoyed swimming and frolicking in the waters of the Toms River.

CONTENTS

Acknowledgments   6

Introduction   7

1.   The River   9

2.   Toms River   33

3.   Island Heights   67

4.   South Toms River   81

5.   Beachwood   93

6.   Pine Beach   105

7.   Ocean Gate   117

ACKNOWLEDGMENTS

Our appreciation is extended to the following persons for their assistance with photographs and information used in the preparation of this publication: Mark Autenrieth and James Simonsen, Ocean County Engineering Department; Edward Beck, Ocean Gate; Geoffrey Brown, Beachwood; Jean Pasqua, Ocean County Map Room; Elinor Bryant, Lakewood; Betty Jane Garthwaite, Berkeley; Louise Hottenstein, Pine Beach; Commodore Charles Kaba, Toms River Yacht Club; Cynthia Kinstler, Toms River; Joyce Kruschwara and Lois Brown, Ocean County Library; Gary Madden, Beachwood; Dorothy Tilton Messineo, Skillman; Marion Stevens, Ocean Gate Historical Society; William Vogel, Toms River; Maude Voigt, Beachwood; and Kay Worth, Berkeley Township. We also thank the volunteer staff of the Richard L. Strickler Research Center of the Ocean County Historical Society for their cooperation during this seven-month-long venture.

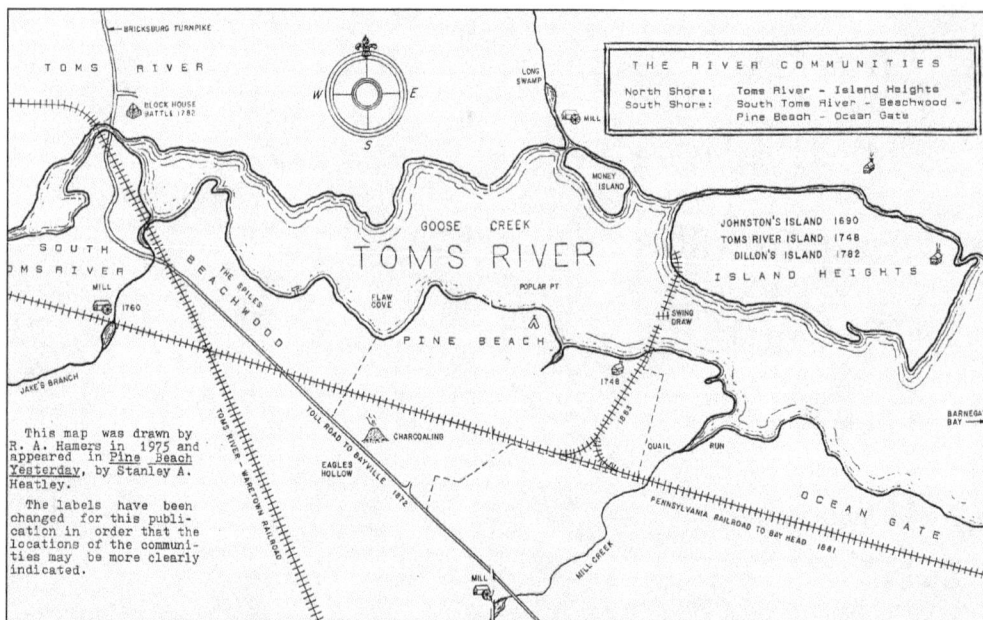

This map was drawn by R.A. Hamers in 1975 for *Pine Beach Yesterday* by Stanley A. Heatley. The labels have been changed for this publication so that the locations of communities may be more clearly indicated.

INTRODUCTION

The beauty of the Toms River remains, despite rapid development along its banks since the completion of the Garden State Parkway in 1955. The part of the river encompassed in this history includes about a 6-mile stretch from the bridge across the Toms River, which links the county seat of Toms River to South Toms River, east to Barnegat Bay.

From the approximate head of tide at the bridge, the river winds peacefully and sinuously toward Barnegat Bay, widening as it flows. It is often called the Toms River Estuary or the Toms River Bay. Geologically speaking, it is a "drowned river." No ugly, drab scars mar its loveliness; fate is not often this kind to our rivers.

Across the bay, nearly opposite the mouth of the river, there was once an opening through the barrier island. It was called Cranberry Inlet. It lasted for many years and was an aid to navigation up the river until it closed about 1812. During the Revolutionary War it was possible for sizable vessels to use it, and as a result, Toms River became a hideout for privateers. Their depredations and capture of British ships incurred the anger of local Tory sympathizers as well as the British. An expedition resulted in the capture of Toms River and the destruction of the local salt works in March 1782. The defenders of the rude blockhouse under Captain Joshua Huddy were overwhelmed, and most of the village was burned. Subsequently, Huddy, a staunch patriot, was hanged illegally by avenging Tories. This caused an international incident which effected the Peace of Paris (1783).

The Van Hise family was photographed aboard their catboat, docked at the rear of stores that fronted on Water Street. This image was made from a tintype which belonged to Alma Van Hise Lillie, who was one hundred years old in 1995.

West of the bridge, the tributaries of the Toms River fan out far and wide making it the second longest canoeable river in the Pinelands. The Toms River drainage basin comprises 167.51 square miles, roughly three times the size of Cedar Creek, the next largest of the little rivers within the confines of Ocean County.

Histories of most of the towns along the river are available, but this is the first pictorial history for the whole Toms River Estuary, which has been compared to a lake of great scenic beauty binding together the towns of Toms River, Island Heights, South Toms River, Beachwood, Pine Beach, and Ocean Gate.

From the mists of time, Thomas Luker emerges as the early settler whose name graced the river (1712) and saved it from the earlier common name of Goose Creek. There are no pictures of Luker's Ferry, which preceded the building of a bridge, nor of his Native American wife. No cameras existed to photograph the early fishermen, pirates, privateers, patriots, Tories, hunters, shipbuilders, charcoalers, and farmers, either. However, over the past twenty-four years the Ocean County Historical Society has catalogued a large collection of prints, as well as sketches and other artistic endeavors relating to the Toms River. There are pictures, for example, of the railroad bridge from Pine Beach to Island Heights.

Hopefully, residents, old and new, as well as tourists, will delight in a pictorial feast of Victorian and Edwardian proportions. Perhaps, this book will enhance a "sense of place" along the Toms River.

The Publications Committee
January 1996

Katherine Gallagher Marston enjoys a ride on this unique chair and sleigh combination in 1903 on frozen Robbins Cove. Houses along Water Street are in the background.

One

THE RIVER

The river on its course to Barnegat Bay, c. 1960. The coves, points of land, curving beaches, and ever-widening stream combine to make a lovely scene. The narrow creek above the town of Toms River flows under the Garden State Parkway and winds its way past Giberson's row of houses, the A.B. Newbury Company, under the Jersey Central tracks, and around Huddy Park. Then its volume of fresh water mixes with the salt water brought in by the tides as it passes Toms River residences, Money Island, and Island Heights on the north shore. On the south shore people in South Toms River, Beachwood, Pine Beach, a bit of Berkeley Township, and the west end of Ocean Gate enjoy its beauty before it enters Barnegat Bay.

This bucolic scene was photographed west of the South Main Street bridge. The swift-running creek, which has wound its way for miles through the Pinelands, suddenly widens, divides its channel, and flows on both sides of the island which is Huddy Park. This causes it to slow its pace as it meets the estuary of the river. This boatman of long ago seems to be adrift on an almost motionless expanse of water. The view is looking toward the Riverside House and a row of boat sheds which back up to the South Main Street bridge.

Located at the head of the navigable portion of the river, this row of boathouses faced the South Main Street bridge. The area behind them is currently a parking lot between the Jersey Central Railroad tracks and Water Street.

Robbins Cove is between Robbins Parkway and Riverview Point. In this c. 1910 view, looking east across the cove, the Marston family's boathouse, the gazebo on the point, and Cedar Point (across the river) are visible.

Snow blanketed the waterfront along Water Street in the 1920s. The Riverview Hotel, the large building with a cupola at the foot of Hooper Avenue on Riverview Point, attracted many local patrons and out-of-town visitors. The John Manning Birdsall boathouse is in the foreground.

Shortly after Edward G. Crabbe (1872–1953) arrived in Toms River in 1900, he formed the Double Trouble Company, which operated a sawmill and cranberry bogs on Cedar Creek. In today's Double Trouble State Park, which encompasses his vast land holdings, the sawmill has been restored for historic purposes. The bogs are tended and harvested each year for the Ocean Spray Cranberry Company. His avocation was boating, which earned him the title of Captain Crabbe. His bright blue yacht, the *Gulf Stream*, carried him from Manasquan to the Gulf of Mexico. Marion McEwan Crabbe, his wife, was president of the Dover Township Board of Education for many years.

This image, called the *Village of Tom's River*, was done in 1861. The spires of the recently-built Presbyterian Church (at Horner and Washington Streets) and the Methodist Episcopal Church (to the right at Hooper Avenue and Washington Street) hover over the village. The other buildings were probably along Water Street.

The arrival of bass in the river brought out fishermen by the dozens. The shad run in the spring produced the same results.

The Island Heights boardwalk extended eastward from the Pennsylvania Railroad station to the pavilion at the foot of Central Avenue. Beachwood and Ocean Gate also built boardwalks along their riverfronts.

These ice boaters were photographed off Island Heights, *c.* 1905. The broad expanses of the bay and the lower part of the river make for good boating, but our latitude and proximity to the ocean do not provide good ice very often. However, when the ice forms, the boats come. Dixon Kemp wrote in his *Manual of Yacht-Boat Sailing* (1886): ". . . those who have experienced the extraordinary velocity of an ice yacht say that when the first dread of the lightning-like flight is overcome, the longing for the fast traveling of an ice yacht becomes quite a fascination."

This is a *c.* 1903 photograph of catboats at their winter mooring along Huddy Park. This part of the river seldom has any ice on it because the current of the narrower creek above the town is so swift.

The Phillips family is shown here aboard the *Lizard*. The children are Stewart, Taylor Rickey, and Virginia Russell Phillips. Mrs. Percy P. Phillips, Mrs. Richard T. Phillips, and Mrs. Wilhelmina M. Phillips are the ladies. The boat is docked behind the stores that fronted on Water Street. Across the main channel of the river is what may have been one of the passenger vessels that plied the waters between Toms River and Seaside Park.

Prior to 1895, Huddy Park was a swampy area. Ralph B. Gowdy bought the swampland and filled it with soil from the hill north of Water Street, and Jefferson Thompson added top soil from his Lakehurst Road farm. In 1905 Mr. Gowdy sold the island to the township for $3,000 so public docking could be provided all around the island. A park with the gazebo (or bandstand) was created in 1907. The gazebo was erected by George Gaskill and members of the Reliance Band. In 1928 the state legislature authorized the erection of a monument to commemorate the defense of the blockhouse. The Joshua Huddy Chapter of the Daughters of the American Revolution gave Huddy Park its name in 1931.

Captain William Pickering Kirk, born in 1835, came to Toms River in 1883. He initially purchased the Moses Applegate farm and started a poultry business in the north end of town, but eventually he turned to shipbuilding, taking over a firm started by his son, John P. Kirk. William Kirk built many of the catboats that sailed Barnegat Bay. He built a 72-by-30-foot schooner here, the largest craft launched locally since the days when coastal schooners were built in the area, as well as craft up to 100 feet long, with a draught of 5 feet. Many of these boats were built for use in the lower Mississippi, along the Gulf Coast, and in Florida waters. Kirk died in Toms River on August 16, 1911.

The *Daisy Memphis* was launched *c.* 1904. William P. Kirk, builder of this boat, advertised in the *New Jersey Courier* of October 4, 1894, as follows: "All classes of sailing and steam yachts constructed from the latest designs. Spars for sale in the rough or finished in first-class manner. Yachts for sale or to hire. Pure manila rope. Crockett's Spar Varnish. Best copper paints. White lead, oils, mixed paints, etc. I sell and use only the Best."

16

Huddy Park, the rounded piece of land on the right, was created to provide additional docking space for boats. About one dozen can be seen tied up at the edge of the park, and another group is visible at the bottom left edge of this *c.* 1900 photograph. In the distance is the tree-covered southern shore of the river, which is now part of the borough of South Toms River. In 1900 it was a virtually uninhabited stretch of land.

After the Civil War, wealthy New Yorkers came to the Toms River area in the summers and bought boats to use for recreation. By 1867 these men had formed a "sailing club" and were competing in races. This club became the Toms River Yacht Club, the second oldest yacht club in the country. At the first meeting, held on July 1, 1871, Charles S. Haines was elected commodore. The club's purposes included encouraging yacht building, recreation, and the cultivation of naval science.

Racing sailboats has been a sport on the Toms River and Barnegat Bay for well over one hundred years. The first organized regatta, won by Job Falkinburg of Forked River, was held on July 27, 1871. The catboats raced from Long Point, at the mouth of the river, to a marker off Forked River and back. This same course was used until 1880 when the railroad bridge to Seaside Park was built. The winner was awarded the Challenge Cup, a trophy which cost $179 and was made of coin silver. Designed by Joseph Schattelier, a New York jeweler who summered at the Ocean House, it was crafted by Tiffany Jewelers. The cup is owned by the Toms River Yacht Club and is one of the oldest perpetual racing trophies in the United States.

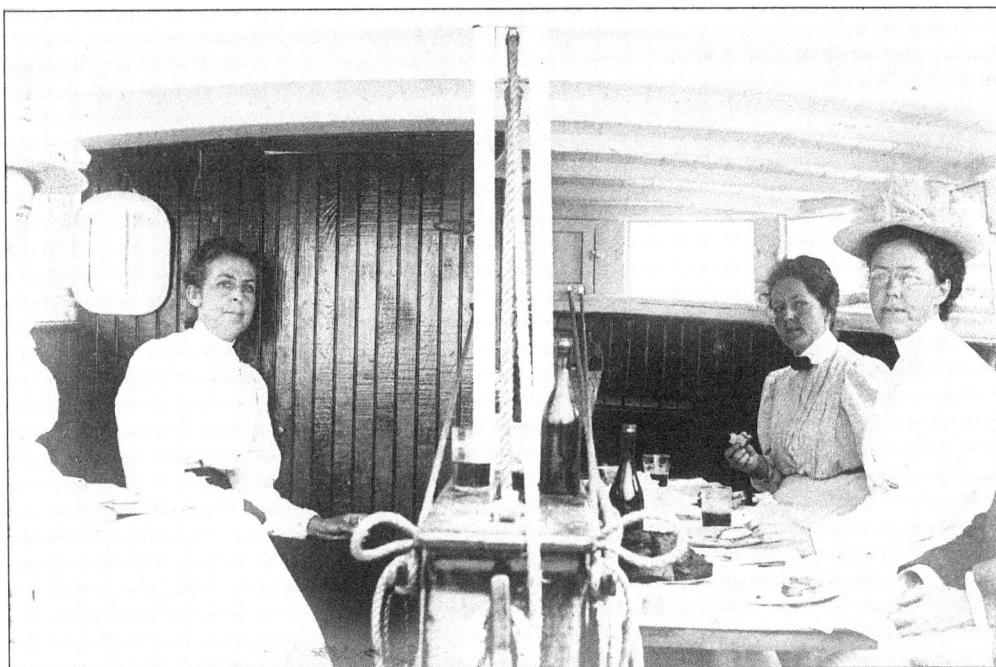

The catboat probably developed on Barnegat Bay as early as the eighteenth century as a means of transportation for families in this part of New Jersey. The first stagecoach between Philadelphia and Tuckerton didn't begin service until 1816. To get from Toms River or any place along Barnegat Bay to Philadelphia or New York, travel by water was the best method. Even to cross to the barrier islands a boat was a necessity. Consequently, the catboats, usually about 30 feet long with a broad beam, had interior cabin space that was considered quite remarkable. The interior of the Marston family's catboat is shown here.

One can't help but wonder about the destination of this nicely-dressed and "well-hatted" family and their two dogs, c. 1880. Someone is visible on the dock behind the mast, holding a line as if to cast off once the skipper is ready and the picture has been taken.

This is *A-cats on the Toms River off Good Luck Point* by Virginia Perle. Four A-cats were built in successive years by Morton Johnson of Bay Head: the *Mary Ann* (1922), the *Bat* (1923), the *Spy* (1924), and the *Lotus* (1925). The *Wasp*, which was added to the fleet in 1982 by David Beaton & Sons, was built on the plans of the original *Tamwock*, which burned in 1941. These boats have been registered as historic landmarks and continue to race on the river and bay each summer. To win the Toms River Challenge Cup is the goal of every A-cat skipper and crew. In this scene the boats are racing on the Wanamaker Course at the mouth of Toms River in Barnegat Bay. The course extends from Island Heights to Seaside Park, from Ocean Gate to the bridge across the bay. In *Sailing Craft* (1928), Edwin J. Schoettle described the catboat as follows: "The catboat is similar in many ways to the one-cylinder motor. A two-, four-, or six-cylinder motor can miss or have one or more cylinders out of commission and still run. The single cylinder motor, however, has to run perfectly or not at all; there is no halfway performance possible. This type of boat has only one sail and there must be perfect harmony between sail and hull."

Money Island is on the north side of the river, about midway between the town of Toms River and the mouth of the river at the east end of Island Heights. It has high bluffs on the river side, similar to those found in Island Heights to the east and in Cranmoor Manor to the west. Legends tell of the famous Captain William Kidd, who reportedly sailed up the river and buried some of his treasure there—thus the name.

Barnegat Bay has been and still is noted for producing some of the best small-boat sailors in the country. The waters are shallow, the winds are good, and the temperature is right—most of the year. The Toms River has numerous yacht clubs along its shores—yacht clubs which have conducted sailing programs for children for many decades. This enables children to grow up in a climate of winds, tides, sails, rigging, sailing tactics, and friends. For many, sailing becomes a way of life. Consequently, sailors at regattas might range in age from eight to eighty.

This 1905 view shows a bit of Huddy Park and the rear of buildings facing Water Street. The first boat on the left bears the name *Ashumet* on its stern. It belonged to Dr. Edwin Ill of Island Heights. The large boat at the right with its bow toward the shed probably belonged to Mayor Weaver.

Residents of the south shore communities often went to Toms River by boat to take care of their business and to shop, since Beachwood, Pine Beach, and Ocean Gate had very few stores in which to buy the staples needed. Boats were docked along Huddy Park and behind the Water Street businesses for the few hours necessary to complete one's transactions.

This Marston youngster is taking his two dogs for an imaginary ride in the family's rowboat, which is still securely tied. The Dover House is at the right. Houses along Robbins Parkway extend to the left.

Ice skating was a popular sport, but during some winters only a few days of good skating were possible. Here Katie Marston and friends enjoy the ice near Riverview Point. The current of the creek delayed freezing near the bridge and Kirk's Boat Works in Toms River. The river iced over more quickly downriver off Pine Beach and Cranmoor Manor.

One of the occupations open to young men living along the river and bay in 1893, for which no capital was necessary, was oystering. This could progress from individual harvesting to a full career. After the Civil War, oyster dredge boats were introduced: oysters were "drudged" from river or bay bottoms, hauled in and separated into different grades by the boat crew, and then shipped by rail to Philadelphia and New York.

Clamming, like oystering, was a traditional sport and occupation along the river and bay. The garvey, a type of boat, was used for "tonging" large quantities of clams. The sneakbox (shown here), a boat developed along Barnegat Bay, was used by an individual clammer, who would generally jump over in shallow water and feel for clams with his feet.

Captain Hazelton Seaman of West Creek is credited with conceiving the design and the construction of the sneakbox in 1836. It was the ideal boat for wild fowl gunners: it could be rowed or sailed in shallow water, could carry the necessary decoys, was completely decked over except for a small cockpit, and could be concealed by covering it with meadow grass or branches. Through the 160 years of its existence, its size, construction, materials, sails, and even its chief purpose have changed. Today it's a racing craft and also a prized possession if its hull is of wood.

The Money Island Yacht Club, begun in 1908, flourished until 1972, when it merged with the Toms River Yacht Club. Money Island families who then joined the Toms River Yacht Club included the Antis, Braun, Callahan, Carlton, Davies, Dirschauer, Endriss, Jasper, Kinstler, Matteo, Moore, Peets, Pollinger, Montague, Renk, Rinzler, Rowbotham, Rudkin, Terhune, Torpey, Warner, White, Whittle, Wilson, and Wright families.

This is a sneakbox of the mid-1900s.

In this old photograph one can readily see why this boat was described as a "box." The waterways of the Jersey shore were on the migratory route of geese, ducks, and brant.

The *Bouquet*, one of two catboats introduced into Barnegat Bay in 1900, influenced the design and construction of future cats built for speed. Amos Lewis of Forked River built the *Bouquet*, and Edward Shoettle bought the *Scat*, which had been built in Osterville, Massachusetts. Both handily defeated all competitors until the Herreshoff-built *Merry Thought* arrived in Barnegat Bay. William Giberson of South Toms River was the owner of the *Bouquet*, c. 1905.

The E-scow was a class of racing sloop sanctioned by the Barnegat Bay Yacht Racing Association in 1924. The Chance brothers, Edwin and Mitchell, were instrumental in introducing the E-scow to this area. The present large fleet of E-scows can be seen racing on the bay every Saturday during the summer, and every yacht club yard along the river has its row of E-scows on trailers waiting for the next race. In the 1920s the scow was considered the fastest boat of its size that had been developed, due primarily to its hull form.

The *Ariella* steam launch, shown on the Toms River, was built at the Kirk's Boat Works about 1913 for Ira Lambert. The name was derived from the reversal of Ira's name and that of his wife Ella. The inset shows a 1916 ticket for a moonlight cruise.

The *Dorianna*, the sister ship of the *Ariella*, was also built at Kirk's for Ira Lambert for river excursion work. This boat was named for Lambert's son, Theodore (nicknamed "Dori"), and Theodore's wife Anna. These boats carried passengers between the various villages along the river and to Seaside Park on Island Beach.

In the foreground, sleek passenger vessels are docked at facilities belonging to Kirk's Boat Works. Docked across the channel of the river, which is divided here by Huddy Park, are the tug *A.D. Wescoat* of Atlantic City and a U.S. Navy barge. Materials from the U.S. Naval Air Station at Lakehurst were being moved out due to the closing of the lighter-than-air program in 1961. In the background are businesses along Route 9 and Flint Road in South Toms River: the Toms River Motor Company, a diner, a feed mill, and a tire shop.

This Elco Cruiser was photographed at Huddy Park, Toms River, in August 1914. At the turn of the century, the majority of watercraft found on the Toms River were sailing vessels, predominately catboats and sneakboxes. However, soon the power boat began to enter the scene.

Salt hay, a natural plant of the marshlands, had many uses: it provided bedding for animals; fertilizer for farmers; insulation for foods being transported and for ice storage houses; stuffing for upholstered seats in Mr. Ford's cars; and the raw materials for brown bags. Scows such as the one in this c. 1900 photograph transported salt hay to markets in Philadelphia, Trenton, and Newark, and to rail connections for New York markets.

Vegetables grown on the mainland were sometimes taken across the bay to Island Beach in wagons, where they were peddled to the fishermen, life-saving crews, and hotel keepers. This is a c. 1900 photograph.

30

The toll bridge across the bay to Seaside Heights was built by the Island Heights and Seaside Heights Bridge Company and opened on December 1, 1915, at a cost of $153,447.90. Tolls varied: a horse and buggy cost 25¢, with each extra person costing an additional 10¢; two horses and a driver cost 40¢; pleasure carts with drivers cost 40¢, with each additional person adding 15¢; all children under five years of age were free; horses, cattle, hogs, and sheep led or in droves each cost 10¢; and a wheelbarrow and one person cost 10¢.

Little is known about the *Chippewa*. This picture was taken about 1895, possibly at Seaside Park. Only two persons are identified—Elizabeth Sammons and Dr. Jump. The group on board are dressed as if on a Sunday afternoon outing.

Photo by Fred Thornes
Toms River, N. J.

This is a delightful scene looking westward up the river. Beginning at the lower left corner on the south shore is a tiny cluster of buildings of the ship-to-shore radio station. Then comes Ocean Gate with its two piers and sandy beaches. Beyond the white patch of sand is a bit of Berkeley Township. Then Pine Beach, Beachwood, and South Toms River can be seen. Where the river is no longer visible, near the top of the photograph, there is a line extending from left to right—the Garden State Parkway. On the right from the lower corner is the long shoreline of Gilford Park and Island Heights. Long Point serves as a dividing point between the river and the bay. Then comes the Island Heights riverfront. The large indentation farther up the river is made by two coves, one on each side of Money Island. The river narrows even more as it passes Cranmoor Manor and the golf course. Dover Township, including Toms River, reaches along the top edge and to the right edge of the photograph.

32

Two

TOMS RIVER

Main Street of Toms River is shown here, *c.* 1915. Along with Water and Washington Streets, this was the heart of a thriving community. On the east side of Main were Roberts's plumbing supply, Singleton's restaurant and ice cream parlor, Schwartz's meat market, Sarah Lewis's Union House (Aunt Sade's rooming house), the Lucien Gravatt residence (with a shoemaker underneath), Joseph Grover's general store, Logan Cowperthwaite's dry goods store, A. Jackson Irons' bakery, Lipschuetz Dry Goods, and Charles Elwell's ice cream parlor. The post and sign at the lower left directed one to "Keep Right."

The town of Toms River, a part of Dover Township, developed in the 1700s on the banks of the Toms River, just before it widens on its way to Barnegat Bay. This c. 1950 view, looking to the northeast, shows the borough of South Toms River, with its lumber yard, feed mill, and other business sites on the south shore of the river. The much larger community of Toms River, the county seat of Ocean County, is on the north shore. Boat yards, a yacht club, the Riverview Hotel, the courthouse complex, and the school plant are visible.

Washington Street is shown here looking from west to east. Horse-drawn buggies provided transportation for those having business "in town." The Presbyterian church stands by itself in the right background. The courthouse can't be seen but is on the left, beyond the church. No wonder the townspeople in 1850 thought that it was being built too far from the center of town.

34

OCEAN HOUSE

Date

The Telegraph-Herald, Printers, Dubuque, Iowa, U. S. Pat., Sept. 19, 1899, Canadian Pat., July 30, 1901.

TIME	ROOM	WEDNESDAY, JULY 8, 1908	RESIDENCE
4.00	B	H 1 Obrholtzer	Philadelphia
		Horace Sprague	Bamegat N J
		N. O S Havens	Pt Pleasant N J
		Joshua Millard M. D.	Manahawkin N J

This is a part of the Ocean House register sheet for July 8, 1908. The Ocean House hosted guests from near and far. Those with business at the county court or in the town often needed to stay overnight because they sometimes traveled from as far as New Egypt, Tuckerton, Manahawkin, or Beach Haven. In the 1870s T.F. Rose, the artist and engraver who came to Toms River from Camden to visit shore sites and prepare sketches for the *Woolman and Rose Atlas* (1878), stayed at the Ocean House.

The Ocean House is shown here, *c.* 1910. This hotel at the northwest corner of Main and Water Streets hosted many distinguished guests. Early names associated with the ownership of this hotel from 1783 to 1803, when it operated as a tavern, were Ivins Davis, Abel Akins, and Tom Barkalow. Abel Akins was a signer of New Jersey's ratification of the U.S. Constitution. The first Ocean County Freeholders' meeting was held at the Ocean House on May 8, 1850. The original portion of the building was moved and became part of a restaurant called the Tavern, which now operates on North Main Street.

The prominent buildings in this c. 1928 photograph are the original Ocean County Courthouse (on the left) and the Hall of Records, added in 1926 (on the right). To the far right is a small white building which housed the Ocean County Library, the county superintendent of schools' office, and other county offices. To the left is the Sheriff's House, built in 1851, the same year as the courthouse. It contained living quarters for the sheriff's family in the front and ten jail cells in the rear. For twenty years this was more than adequate since there were seldom more than two prisoners at a time and usually not more than a dozen each year! Nevertheless, the house was built with a belfry bell, which was sounded to alert the villagers to an escape. (Today a dormer window occupies that spot, and the bell is now in the belfry of the Cedar Grove Methodist Church on Bay Avenue and Cedar Grove Road.) In 1921 twenty-four new jail cells were added in a wing at the rear of the building (visible in the aerial photograph on p. 37). The Greek Revival courthouse with its imposing Doric columns was built soon after the first governing body selected the site of Joseph Coward's cornfield for its erection in 1850. Mr. Coward then donated 6,000 bricks for the project. These bricks were shipped from Haverstraw, New York, by schooner, unloaded at Robbins Cove, and taken up the hill by wagon. By September 1851 the building was complete, and county business was conducted under one roof. The old cornfield had become the center of a city block, bounded by Horner, Hooper, Sheriff, and Washington Streets. The Hall of Records from 1926 to 1950 housed the county clerk on the first floor and had a court room and law library on the second floor. A second-floor bridge connected the new court room with the one in the original building. In 1950 this building was torn down to make way for a whole new east wing. (You can notice in the following photograph that the columned building next to the courthouse is gone.) Both the courthouse and the Sheriff's House were placed on the National Register of Historic Places in 1983.

This 1980s aerial photograph is testimony to the massive growth of the county in little more than a century. The courthouse with its columns is easy to find as is the Sheriff's House behind it, but two additions have been made to the west wing of the courthouse (on the left). The first was added in 1950 to house the county clerk's office, after the old Hall of Records was torn down. The second addition, in 1974, provided space for the surrogate and small claims courts. Meanwhile, to the right of the courthouse, the east wing expansion had progressed and, to the first addition made in 1950, a 1965 building was added. All of this meant new court rooms and space for the increasing number of judges. Behind the east wing, jail space was added in 1961. This expansion added capacity for 110 inmates and was used in conjunction with the old 1921 wing of the Sheriff's House. Space for the probation and sheriff's department was also provided here. Even this addition was soon inadequate for the burgeoning county population. Although it does not appear in this photograph, in 1985 a fourth jail with 196 cells was added to the north of the courthouse, along with seven new court rooms. This new facility is called the Justice Complex. There has been other county construction in the area since this photograph was taken, but it clearly indicates what has become of Mr. Coward's cornfield!

Churches, Toms River, N. J.

1 Presbyterian
2 Baptist
3 Methodist
4 Catholic
5 Episcopal

These Presbyterian, Baptist, Methodist, Catholic, and Episcopal churches, among the earliest in Toms River, were photographed c. 1909. The Methodists, organized in 1828, had two earlier buildings, all at the intersection of Hooper and Washington Streets. The Presbyterians started a church in 1852 and erected a building in 1858. The Baptists, organized in 1867, built a church on the corner of Main and Broad Streets in 1895. A Catholic church was built in 1882 on Hooper Avenue next to the Methodist Cemetery; pictured here is their second church, dating from 1904. The Episcopal Church was founded in 1865, and in 1873 they bought a building on Hooper Avenue for $400; the church shown here was built between 1882 and 1885 on land donated by John P. Haines.

The 1858 Presbyterian church survives in downtown Toms River as a meeting room in the Ocean County Library complex on Washington Street. Its bell, installed by the township, still tolls the hours, and its tall steeple remains a landmark. In its 137 years the building has undergone many facade changes. This is how it looked about 1900.

Cranmoor Farm was the home of John Peter Haines. Mr. Haines proved to be an excellent farmer even though he was a "city boy." His herd of Jersey cattle, which he personally selected, was said to be unexcelled by any in the United States. The farm consisted of several barns (one of which housed his automobile collection), a greenhouse, a windmill, and a gristmill. The name Cranmoor is carried on today in the residential area known as Cranmoor Manor. It is on the bluffs overlooking the river to the east of the golf course.

John Peter Haines was born in 1831 to William and Emily Stagg Haines. John joined his father, who was a wealthy New York City merchant, in the mercantile business until shortly after his marriage to Mary Merritt, at which time he purchased 100 acres along the Toms River. He named his home there Cranmoor Farms. Soon after acquiring the land, Mr. Haines donated a portion to Christ Episcopal Church. The congregation still worships in the church built on that land.

Toms River Volunteer Fire Company #1 was organized on January 1, 1896, with twenty-two members. Funds were raised to build an engine house on Horner Street under the township's water tank. Shown here is the first hook and ladder truck, c. 1905. An earlier fire company had been formed by the Magnolia House management in 1870 because of their concern for the safety of their new hotel. It was known as the "Hook, Ladder and Bucket Company."

The Reliance Band, associated with Volunteer Fire Company #1, was the first band organized in Toms River. They played under an arc light several times a week at the corner of Washington and Main Streets, until the gazebo was erected in Huddy Park in 1908. Some of the men identified in this early 1900s photograph are Charles Berrien, Elmer Doxsey, Roland Buckwalter, Chillion and Phillip Applegate, Lester Yoder, Sam and William Pierce, Tom Gaskill, Cy Yates, Martin and Babe Schwartz, and Owen Shutts.

40

The Village School on Horner Street in Toms River was a 281-by-361-foot, two-story building with two classrooms. It was constructed in 1854 at a cost of $349.47 to replace an earlier schoolhouse. An addition in 1870 gave the school a new front and provided rooms for the primary, intermediate, grammar, and high schools. In 1882 the enrollment reached 172. After a new school (see below) was built across the street in 1900, this building held some classes for awhile, was then used as an opera house, and was later converted into a bowling alley.

The attractive Toms River School, built in 1900, made it possible for the students of the Village School to move across the street into eleven new classrooms (two more remained unfinished for a year). Two teachers, one of whom was Miss Laura Gowdy (head of the French department), composed the high school faculty that first year. This building served as the high school from the 1920s until Toms River High School South replaced it in the 1960s. For a few years after that it again housed elementary school students; it is now used for administrative offices.

41

This c. 1913 photograph shows the Germania School, one of eight one-room schoolhouses in the area in the early 1900s. It was located near the intersection of Lakehurst Road and Route 37 and was typical of area schools. Miss Mary E. Redmond (the teacher) can be seen in this photograph, as well as: (front row) Nelson Lee, Raymond Thompson, Samuel Norcross, Elwood Thompson, Abe Gant, Bill Lee, Russell Thompson, and Norman McKelvey; (back row) May Luker, Eva Luker, Edna Thompson (the tiny girl), Myrtle Fleming, Stella Luker, Adeline Luker, and George and Thomas Luker.

The beautiful Toms River Grade School on Hyers Street was added to the school campus in 1923. It provided rooms for students from kindergarten through the eighth grade, and also provided a clinic, cafeteria, manual training shop, library, and art department to be used by all pupils, including those of the high school. The gymnasium, auditorium, and several classrooms were added to the back of the building in 1928. When it was deemed unsafe in the 1980s it was razed.

42

These three vehicles, shown here c. 1925, were used to bring the students from the areas formerly served by the one-room schools to the town school. Beginning in 1870, some high school courses were taught at the Village School, but children who completed grade eight and passed the qualifying examination in an outlying school often found it difficult or impossible to attend high school classes. Dover Township, covering a 42-mile area, is the fifth largest district in New Jersey and has the largest bus fleet in the state.

The Dover Township School Board in Toms River during 1913–14 consisted of the following members, from left to right: Corson McKelvey; A. Hudson Harris, district clerk; Charles R. Berrien; W. Howard Jeffrey, president; Charles L. Tilton Jr.; Dr. Ralph R. Jones; Harry E. Toner; and Theodore Fischer. At that time, Island Heights, Seaside Park, Seaside Heights, Beachwood, Pine Beach, Ocean Gate, South Toms River, and the Berkeley and Lacey Townships all sent students to the Toms River High School.

Albert S. Tilton (1863–1929), a Toms River school principal, is second from the right. His thirty-five year career in education began in Dover Chapel, and he was one of the few educators in the county who held a Professional Certificate, the highest certificate the state offered.

In the top row are the school (1900), the annex (1914), and the grade school (1923). In the center is the vocational building, which housed carpentry and auto mechanics shops, classrooms, and an area for students of home economics and family relationships. At the bottom are a cottage and the "B Flat," the home of the music department. The opening of Toms River High School South made all of these, except for the vocational building, unnecessary.

44

George Woodward Cowperthwaite was born March 7, 1825, in New Egypt. In 1856 he built the two-story Cowperthwaite Exchange building on Main Street, which has been used by businesses, churches, and fraternal organizations through the years. Until the 1930s the post office occupied a corner of the first floor. Other business interests of Mr. Cowperthwaite included real estate, farming, cranberry culture, charcoal shipping, shipbuilding, and newspaper publishing.

Gravestones on display were a familiar sight on Washington Street in the early to mid-twentieth century. Isaac W. Richtmeyer's monument business was wedged in between larger buildings, one of which was Charney's Stationery Store. Mr. Richtmeyer, a stone cutter from New York, came to Toms River to recover his health about 1900. He purchased the William Farr monument business, then located on Water Street. His daughters were Grace (who married Roy Tilton), Ruth (who married Frank Sutton), and Maude (who remained single).

The west side of Main Street included, from left to right: the Federal-style house owned by Maja Leon Berry, the Ocean County Trust Company, the Cowperthwaite Exchange (which housed the post office). The Ocean County Trust building, erected in 1928 for the sum of $165,000, later became the home of the First National Bank, which expanded to include the Exchange. Note the horse-watering trough in front of the post office.

This lovely Italian-style mansion named "Springside" on Washington Street was built in 1867 by Washington Hadley. It contained twenty rooms, some of which were 32 feet long with 12-foot-high ceilings. In 1873, at a sheriff's sale, the house was purchased by the Willets family, who, in turn, sold it to William F. Mott in 1884 for $12,000. The house was demolished in 1978.

46

Mrs. M.E. Beatty and Charrie Hooper, her daughter by a previous marriage, are shown here *c*. 1869 at the home of Joseph Francis, the inventor of the armored car and a life-saving boat. Mrs. Beatty was the daughter of sea captain George W. Giberson. Mr. Beatty was active in the Toms River Yacht Club and had a catboat named for his step-daughter, the *Charrie H*.

The Magnolia House formally opened to the public on July 11, 1870, with a celebrated orchestra from New York providing the entertainment. It was built by the Building and Improvement Company of Hudson County, which hoped to attract wealthy New Yorkers and Philadelphians to the area. By the turn of the century the hotel business dwindled and part of the hotel fell to the wrecker's ball. The Keswick Colony of Mercy in Whiting used some of the lumber to construct their administration building. The remaining portion still stands on the original tract.

47

The Ocean National Bank, located on the southeast corner of Main and Water Streets, was the third bank established in Toms River, all of which failed. Prior to 1851, merchants traveled by stage to Freehold, the county seat of Monmouth County, to do their banking. The first two banks were the Delaware and Hudson and the Union, both established in 1851. Ocean National opened in 1857, and is shown here c. 1860.

The First National Bank of Toms River opened on March 10, 1881, with John Aumack as its first president and William A. Low as its first cashier. The resources after the first day of business totaled $37,787. The bank occupied the site of the failed Ocean National until it merged with the Ocean County Trust Company in 1944, at which time it moved to a Main Street location. In 1991, after 110 years as one of the leading banks in the area, First National failed and was taken over by First Fidelity.

48

Joseph Lawrence Francis (1801–1893) was an inventor of safety devices for those who went to sea, and he gained worldwide recognition because of his contributions, which saved so many lives. To those along the Jersey shore, where shipwrecks were a frequent occurrence, the galvanized iron life-car was one of his most valuable inventions. By means of the life-car a wrecked ship's passengers and crew could be rescued. Other inventions included a portable screw boat, a molded boat, an anchor launch, a floating dock, a military hood, and the nautilus life preserver.

The Riverview Hotel was formerly the home of Joseph Francis. To quote the *Historical and Biographical Atlas of the New Jersey Coast* (Woolman and Rose, 1878): "We found Mr. Francis at his pleasant country place situated on the banks of the river. Having retired some years since from the active duties of a long and arduous business life, he is now resting, as it were, upon the laurels won by him in the cause of humanity and progress."

Riverview Point, located at the south end of Hooper Avenue, was the site of Joseph Francis's home, which was later converted into the Riverview Hotel. The hotel was a favorite luncheon and dinner spot for local organizations and residents, and it also provided good lodging for visitors. For many years it was under the management of Anna and William Fritz. The old wooden structure was destroyed by fire on Christmas night in 1965. Condominiums are currently located on this site and a marina is located in Hainer Cove, on the east side of Riverview Point.

The home of James G. Gowdy was located at the corner of Washington Street and Clifton Avenue. The Gowdy brothers, Daniel and Ralph, were successful cranberry growers in the county in the mid and late 1800s. Daniel owned the Stafford Forge Plantation near West Creek. Together the brothers planted fifty bogs by contract and sold one hundred and fifty others. This home, built in 1873, was an American Legion Convalescent Center after World War I, and the Hollywood Inn in the 1940s. The Elks Lodge, BPOE #1875, owns it now.

50

Joseph Grover's business was located at 39–41 Main Street. Mr. Grover was the eldest of twelve children of James and Cornelia Wainwright Grover. Joseph was a businessman in Toms River for almost fifty years, first owning a bicycle shop, then a general store, and finally a Willys Overland car dealership. *The New Jersey Courier*, a weekly newspaper, was printed on the second floor of the building. Beginning in the 1930s, Harmony Lodge #18, F & AM, and Gloria Chapter #159, OES, met on the third floor.

Childs' grocery and delivery service was located on Washington Street in 1885. Childs sold, among other things, Naptha Floating Laundry Soap for 10¢, salt pork for 13¢, and tea for 27¢. Large letters under the name "Childs" in each window advertised that they were coffee roasters and tea importers. Note the two different wheel sizes on the wagon.

Amos Birdsall (1829–1909) was born in Waretown. He began a shipbuilding business in Tuckerton that produced four and six-masted schooners. When business dwindled in New Jersey, he moved to Camden, Maine. Upon returning to Toms River, he built a magnificent home on Washington Street. The property on Hadley Avenue on which the Ocean County Historical Society's Museum stands was donated by his heirs. A room in the museum is named in honor of the Birdsall family.

The Marston family home, located at 61 Water Street on the banks of the Toms River, was originally the home of author Nathaniel Holmes Bishop. After his death in 1902, the house was purchased by the Marstons. Frank Marston (on the right) was an insurance broker. His wife Katherine (seated in the rocker), or "Katie" as she was known, was deaf but enjoyed both the family catboat and ice skating on the river. She was an active member of Christ Episcopal Church. Frank died in 1913 and Katherine died in 1941.

A bequest from the estate of Nathaniel Holmes Bishop enabled Dover Township to erect the Bishop Library for the community in 1941. About thirty years later the property of the Presbyterian Church on the opposite corner was acquired by the county. A new library was constructed and the church became a meeting room. Bishop Library, renamed the New Jersey Room, was made part of the county system. It houses reference materials for historical and genealogical research.

Nathaniel Holmes Bishop (1838–1902) was born in Massachusetts and came to Toms River in the 1860s. His was a life of adventure: he traveled in a paper canoe; took a four-month journey in a sneakbox; raised cranberries in Stafford Township; and traveled extensively through the United States and South America. His portrait hangs over the fireplace in this view of the beautifully-decorated interior of the Bishop Library.

Edwin H. Berry left home at an early age because he did not like farming. In 1884 he came to Toms River with L.W. Thurber and bought out the hardware business of John Aumack. In 1885 Mr. Thurber retired from the business and a new partnership of Berry and Frost was formed. In 1893 Mr. Berry bought out Frost and ran the business under his own name until 1926, when he incorporated as Berry's Store. The store was run by his son, Allan H. Berry, until the late 1960s.

These boats were tied up at the rear of the stores on Water Street, c. 1900. This was the head of navigation of the Toms River. Beyond this point upstream the river was, and still is, a narrow winding creek. The buildings shown here are, from left to right: Berry's hardware store, John Hyers' liquor store, and Peanut John's produce store.

The Riverside House was located at the southwest corner of Water and Main Streets, Toms River. Its proprietor, George C. Van Hise, took over the operation in 1896. A livery business was operated at the rear of the hotel.

In this view, looking south from the intersection of Main and Water Streets, the New Jersey Central Railroad trestle is visible in the background to the right. The bulkhead for the trestle was made of logs laid lengthwise. The sign over the road cautioned riders to "Walk Your Horse."

Charles P. Anderson was a ship's carpenter who opened a funeral business in Barnegat in 1869. A decade later he sold his business and moved to Hooper Avenue in Toms River where he started another. His son, C.P. Anderson Jr., took over after his death. This hearse, shown here at the corner of Hooper Avenue and Sheriff Street, was donated to the Ocean County Historical Society and loaned by them to Batsto State Park. Marvin S. Campbell went to work for Anderson in the 1920s and became a partner in 1937, thus creating the Anderson and Campbell business located at 703 Main Street today.

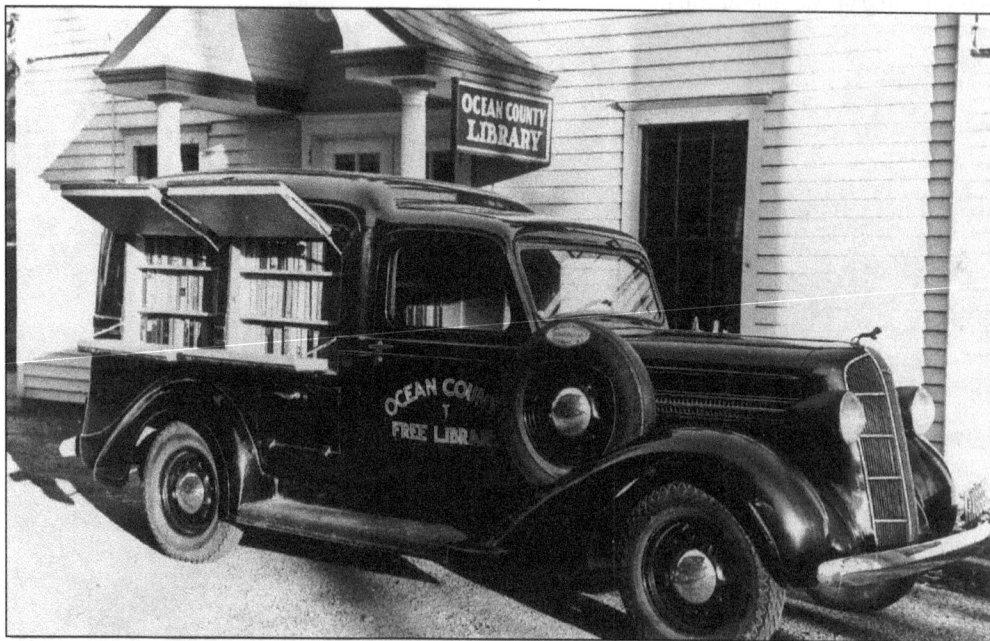

From a modest beginning in the 1920s, the bookmobile grew in size until it was finally retired in 1995. The vehicle that served as the bookmobile carried hundreds of books to schools and small communities in the county on a regular basis. Many schools had no library room, so the bookmobile supplied students with the taste of a library. By the 1990s the branches of the Ocean County Library brought library services to most residents and the bookmobile was no longer needed.

The intersection of Main and Water Streets is shown here in a view looking north from the bridge. On the right corner is the First National Bank, formerly the Ocean National Bank. The building to the left is the Riverside House. The historic Ocean House can be seen on the northwest corner across from the Riverside.

The Ocean House had its beginning in the 1780s, when a small tavern was built for Abel Akins. In 1855 it was sold to Jesse Cowdrick. Cowdrick died in the Civil War, and his wife sold it to her cousin, S. Tuttle Cowdrick, and Britton C. Cook. It operated, c. 1890, as the Cowdrick and Cook Hotel. New owners in 1906 changed the name to the Ocean House.

The "Hole in the Wall," made by connecting buildings on the second floor, allowed traffic to go to and from Washington Street along Hyers Street. Because of the pond that had existed at one time where Hyers Street is located, the street was also known as Frog Alley. Posters in the store window tell about "The Covered Wagon" coming to town. In time this building was torn down and replaced by Woods' Market.

Harris's Restaurant was located on the east side of Main Street on the site of a rooming house which had been razed. To the left of the restaurant was Harris's Cigar and Stationery store. In 1923 this store was purchased by Abraham and Morris Harris, who moved their dry goods business from Water Street. Abe's son Sidney managed the store for many years. Today Sidney's son Glenn and Glenn's wife, Chris, are the proprietors.

This *c.* 1910 photograph documents one of the early horse-drawn sleigh races that took place on Main Street, Toms River, between Union and Dover Streets. Roy Tilton, Dr. Brouwer, and a Mr. Irons were three of the drivers.

The steep conical thatched roof and narrow door of this late 1800s ice house restrained heat. The flooring was several feet below ground level. Saw dust—used for insulation—covered the ice, which generally lasted until the next fall.

These veterans of the Grand Army of the Republic were photographed at the Ocean County Courthouse. During its early years the courthouse was often used for festive occasions, such as the departure of local men for action in the Civil War (Company F, 14th Regiment), and the return of war heroes. Later it hosted assemblages of the GAR and the like. At such times banners were draped between the Doric columns and appropriate exercises held.

At the time of this photograph A.E. Burnside Post #59, GAR, consisted of Gilbert G. ?, James M. Pettet, Edward Smith, Charles L. Tilton, Joseph E. Wainwright, Charles S. Applegate, Shinn C. Jameson, Commander Adolph Ernst, Lawrence Berrien, Richard Walton, Franklin Wilsey, Joseph Walton, Samuel S. Brinley, and Master Adolph Ernst, bugler. Company F, 14th Regiment, consisting of men recruited in Ocean County, was formed in August 1862 with 9 officers and 139 enlisted men. They saw action in the "Wilderness Campaign" and in numerous other battles including Petersburg and Appomattox.

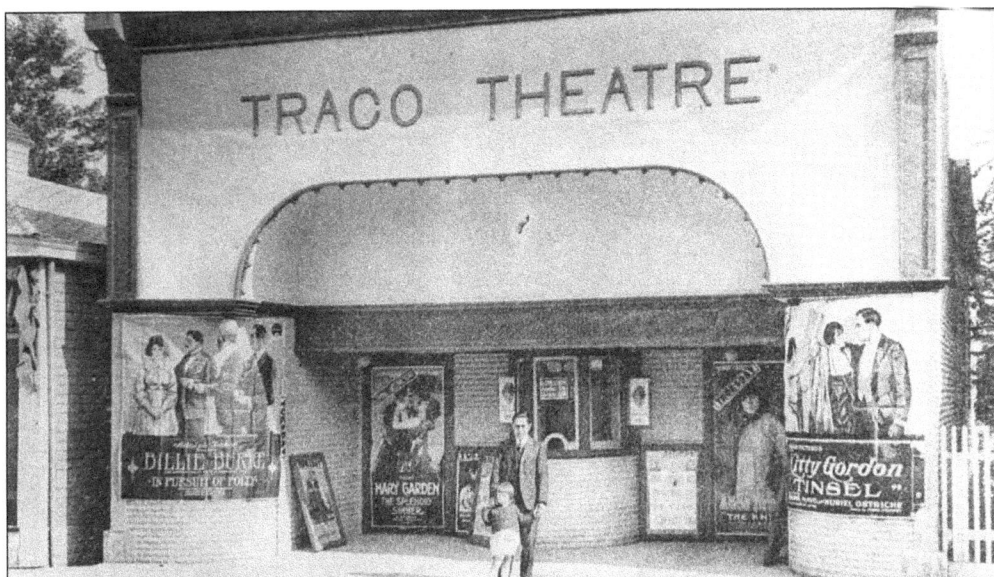

Isadore (Izzy) Hirshblond purchased the Toms River Amusement Company about 1920 and opened the Traco Theater. Standing in front are Mr. Hirshblond and Charlotte Ewart. Saturday morning shows for local children were very popular and well attended in those early days. Vaudeville, circus shows, dance recitals, and newspaper drives were also held here. Stars like Abbott and Costello stopped in and performed on their way to and from New York City. This site is now part of the property of the Sovereign Bank, formerly the Jersey Shore Savings and Loan Association.

The Community Theater, the second movie house on Washington Street, was built in 1937 as a Walter Reade theater. In 1941 it became part of the Toms River Company and was managed by Isadore Hirshblond. It was a gathering place for special events that brought much enjoyment to the community. Free tickets were given at Thanksgiving to the Toms River High School football team, band, cheerleaders, and coaches to celebrate either a win or loss in their game with Lakewood High School. Upon Mr. Hirshblond's death in 1961, the theater reverted to the Walter Reade management.

Thomas A. Mathis (1869–1958) and Maja Leon Berry (1877–1961) were outstanding contemporaries born within a few miles of each other at Tuckerton and West Creek. Mathis became first officer on J.P. Morgan's yacht and commanded the *Columbia*, an America's Cup defender. His career in politics took him to the New Jersey Senate, and he chaired and dominated the Ocean County Republican Party for many years. People spoke of the "TAM machine." After retiring, he owned a Ford dealership, and at the time of his death he was the county treasurer. Berry's first job was that of a teacher. From there he studied law, and at age thirty he was appointed judge of the court of common pleas in Ocean County. Other appointments followed, and in 1947 he became a superior court judge. Selected phrases from his obituary show the esteem in which he was held: "Exemplified ideals upon which this country was founded; outstanding and judicious man both on the bench and as a practicing attorney; innately brilliant; courage and perseverance; worked as a railroad clerk and funded his own college education; was an elder of the Presbyterian Church and taught the Men's Bible Class for thirty-five years." This photograph was taken in Trenton on January 6, 1930.

Heinen Air Yacht #10584 was built by the corporation of that name in Atlantic City in 1930. The airship could seat three in its streamlined car suspended below the envelope. For registration purposes, it was described as a "sporting yacht also for other commercial purposes." The final entry for the air yacht indicates that registration was cancelled in 1935 due to "insurance policy cancellation." The airship is shown here moored behind houses on Park Street.

The crossroads of Locust Street (now Route 37) and Hooper Avenue are shown here in the very early 1930s. The only building at that intersection was Ally Applegate's combination gas station and candy store, which was surrounded by farmland. There is a much larger gas station on the site today; the other three corners of the intersection house a stock brokerage, a jewelry store, and a fast-food business.

Robbins Parkway and Robbins Cove are named after Elijah Robbins, the first postmaster of Toms River and the owner of a tavern on the east side of Main Street. Robbins Parkway is the town's only street (just one block long) with a parkway dividing the traffic lanes.

Main Street, c.1935, was photographed from the second story of Bart's Men's Shop. The businesses visible along the east side of Main Street include the Marion Hotel, Parlin Photo Service, the Candy Land Luncheonette, Purpuri Shoes, the Beacon Restaurant, Harris's department store, the Army and Navy Shop, a bakery, and Ray Drugs. On the west side the Acme Market, a Mobil gas station, and a diner can be seen. Only Purpuri Shoes and Harris's remain at these sites today.

Since Toms River was settled in the early 1700s, it has been the largest community in Dover Township. The township then included land from Oyster Creek to Howell Township but has shrunk in size as new boroughs and townships have been created. The two names, Toms River and Dover, both referring to the same community, prove puzzling to visitors and newcomers even today. The Dover Township's Town Hall was originally the home of Captain John Holmes and was built in 1900 at a cost of $20,000. It later became the residence of Mr. Henry Low, a president of the First National Bank, and is now part of the much larger Dover Township Municipal Building.

Dr. James Marianno Russo, an osteopathic physician who specialized in obstetrics, opened offices at 623 Main Street in the 1940s. Subsequently, he purchased the property of the Halbach Estate, which he converted into the Toms River Maternity Hospital. It was an institution popular throughout the greater Toms River area during the 1950s, because it was the only hospital between Lakewood and Atlantic City until the Community Memorial Hospital opened in 1952.

When veterinarian Henry Clay Glover learned that mange could be treated successfully with a medicine developed by Toms River pharmacist Charles B. Mathis, he contacted Mathis and proposed a union between the two for marketing the "cure." Glover's Mange Cure went into production in 1876, and by 1916 the success of the business allowed the Glover Building, a three-story building at Water and Robbins Streets, to be built. The business closed in 1992 and the building is now the Law Center of Ocean County.

The annual Halloween parade, begun in the 1930s, now attracts over 20,000 people. Store windows along the parade route are painted by high school art students. A long line of costumed entrants of all ages pass in review before judges, who decide the prize recipients. Prominent citizens are chosen to be judges. These judges of the 1953 Halloween Parade are Samuel B. Pierce Sr., Mrs. William Gwyer, Mrs. William B. Pierce, and Isadore Hirshblond.

Three

ISLAND HEIGHTS

Island Heights was established as one of the first camp meeting associations in this area. The auditorium was built in 1879 to accommodate summer worshippers, who numbered between 1,500 and 2,000 at many services. These services often lasted several hours. The auditorium was located on a bluff high above the Toms River, and while it has long since disappeared, the land located on Ocean Avenue is still referred to as "the camp meeting grounds."

SEASON OF 1884.

❖ Island ❖ Heights ❖

BY THE SEA.

This popular watering place and camp meeting ground is located on a *high island*, at the junction of *Island Bay* and *Barnegat Bay, fronting on these waters and also facing the Ocean. Nothing intervenes between Island Heights* and the *Ocean* except the *Bay* and a *sand beach*, which acts as a breakwater and is 300 yards wide. The facilities for bathing in still water or surf are excellent.

There *is no hot land breeze at Island Heights, the southwest winds come to us over the broad waters* of Island Bay, while from the south there is an unobstructed *sea breeze*.

The camp ground is on a *high bluff*, *60 feet above the water line*. Twenty acres of shady forest have been set apart for camp meeting purposes, on the highest and most delightful portion of the Island.

A large number of small cottages have been erected on Camp Ground Square ; these are rented at prices ranging from $15 to $20 for the entire season. The Association also owns a large number of tents that are rented at low rates.

A LARGE AUDITORIUM

seated with Park Settees has been completed in which the religious services are held.

A large room, 28x40, over the pulpit platform, is nicely fitted up as a lodging room for preachers who aid in the meetings.

PROGRAMME FOR 1884.

FOURTH OF JULY CELEBRATION.
S. S. ASSEMBLY, Tuesday, July 29th, to August 4th.
REGULAR CAMP MEETING, August 8th to August 17th.
TEMPERANCE CAMP MEETING, August 21st to August 24th.

RAILROAD FACILITIES.

Trains over the Pennsylvania Railroad run direct to Island Heights from Philadelphia and intermediate points without change of cars. Passengers from New York go over Pennsylvania Railroad via Long Branch and Ocean Grove direct to Island Heights. Island Heights is connected with the Pennsylvania Railroad system, thus securing excellent connection to and from all parts of the country. See time tables.

EXCURSION TICKETS

From Philadelphia to Island Heights, good for two days, $2.20. Season tickets, good until November, $2.75. Coupon books for the season or year at $40 and $50, from Philadelphia. Excursion tickets also from New York, Long Branch, Ocean Grove and intermediate points.

The September 6, 1884 issue of *New Jersey Coast Pilot*, a newspaper, contained this advertisement extolling the attributes of Island Heights, which was founded as a Methodist camp meeting association in 1878.

RECREATION.

While everything tending to immorality is prohibited, innocent recreation is encouraged, and for this Island Heights has nothing to rival it on the Atlantic Coast. Sunday schools, churches and private parties can find no better place for a day's real enjoyment than at Island Heights.

BARNEGAT BAY, with its Fishing, Bathing and Boating,

Opens an endless source of enjoyment to pleasure-seekers.

ISLAND HEIGHTS HAS ONE MILE FRONT ON ISLAND BAY,

the most beautiful bay along our coast. Its waters are pure; its tides are gentle, and its shores are sandy—just the place for small boats as well as yachts.

ISLAND BAY IS THE CHILDREN'S PARADISE.

Here they can bathe and boat in perfect safety.

IMPROVEMENTS.

Wide avenues have been opened, graded and graveled at the expense of the Association. The Association has expended nearly $100,000 in public improvements. There are two excellent hotels—the Island House and the Perennial—besides a number of cottage boarding-houses. There is a large church, in which public services are held regularly during the year. Private enterprise has also expended about a quarter *million* dollars.

INVALIDS

Will find Island Heights a sanitarium. Eminent physicians have recommended invalids to go to Island Heights, on account of its excellent water and air.

A HEALTH RESORT!

LOTS ARE STILL SOLD AT VERY LOW PRICES.

Our place is surrounded by Ocean, Bay and forest; our *drainage is natural* and *perfect;* our water is pure, *cold and delicious.*

For cottages, tents, lots, or any other information, address

REV. J. SIMPSON, Island Heights, N. J.
D. SOMERS RISLEY, ESQ., 106 Market St., Camden, N. J.
CHAS. E. HILL, ESQ., 828 Broad St., Newark, N. J.
JAMES L. HAYS, 749 Broad St., Newark, N. J.

tf

According to the author of the booklet *Island Heights and Windsor Park* (1888): "It is not surprising that everybody who visits Island Heights is pleased with its real beauty of scenery and attractiveness of location."

In 1878 a group of men formed the Island Heights Association and purchased 172 acres of land. In 1887 the borough was established as a "Christian family resort under temperance influences"; these influences remain, and Island Heights is still "dry." No tavern or liquor store licenses have ever been issued. Today the borough of Island Heights consists of 400 acres. The triangle at the lower left was where railroad passengers arrived and departed.

These Victorian houses were located along River Avenue on the eastern shoreline of Island Heights. The old houses sitting on the hilltop overlooking the Toms River have been a familiar sight for many years. In 1982 more than 375 structures in the borough were recorded by a survey team as part of the Historic District and were nominated to be included in the State and National Register of Historic Places.

70

During the first few winters at Island Heights, worship services were held in private homes and at the local hotel, the Island House. The high bluff behind the hotel was the site of the camp meeting grounds.

After the Island House was remodeled, it was renamed the Edgewater Hotel. The hotel was located at the foot of Central Avenue directly across from the bathing beach. The ground floor contained a soda fountain and luncheonette, which was a convenient gathering place for bathers and boaters. The building was destroyed by fire in 1986.

This one-room elementary school, built in 1889 on Summit Avenue by the Reverend John Simpson, was the first school that children of this community attended. In 1897 the school employed only two teachers. In 1904 the whole building was raised and a new first story was built underneath, and in 1913 another room was added at the side. The unusual fire escape, a chute from the upper floor to the ground, was always fun and sometimes a bit scary during fire drills. The building was moved to Route 37 and served as McCormick's farm stand until it burned in 1988.

The Springs was a furniture factory before being converted to the Girls Friendly Holiday House, which was owned and operated by the Episcopal Church of New Jersey as a summer camp for girls. The building was destroyed by fire, and a small housing development currently occupies the site, which is on River Avenue just off West End Avenue.

As Island Heights became known as a summer resort, the need for increased transportation became apparent. A railroad bridge was built across the Toms River in 1883 which connected Island Heights with the main Pennsylvania Railroad line. In 1915, the Pennsylvania Railroad merged with the Pemberton and Hightstown Railroad and the Kinkora and New Lisbon Railroad, to create the Pennsylvania and Atlantic Railroad.

This Island Heights railroad station was built in 1884 along the north bank of the Toms River. Trains would backup from Pine Beach, across the 1,800-foot bridge, to deposit passengers at the passenger station. A 40-foot draw opening permitted boats to pass through while the draw was open. Prior to building the trestle, a ferry operated between Pine Beach and Island Heights. The tracks continued along the west end of Island Heights for about half a mile to a lumber and coal yard. Children from the Germantown (later Pershing) School often picked wildflowers to sell to passengers returning to Philadelphia.

John Wanamaker, owner of the famous Wanamaker's department stores in Philadelphia and New York, purchased several acres along the eastern end of Island Heights and established a summer camp for his employees. Built in 1904, the Wanamaker Commercial Institute Barracks contained a dining hall and barracks for the counselors. The campgrounds and buildings were later sold to the Presbyterian Church, who operated a camp there for a few years. The post office, borough hall, tax office, and police station are currently housed in several buildings on the site.

Wanamaker employees became "cadets" when they spent their two-week summer vacations at the Wanamaker Commercial Institute. A band made up by the cadets played for marching exhibitions, which were enjoyed by many. The building in the background is situated on a bluff overlooking the Toms River and Barnegat Bay.

After trains backed up across the trestle from Pine Beach to Island Heights, passengers disembarked and headed for the Edgewater Hotel or just strolled on the boardwalk. When this *c*. 1910 photograph was taken, horse-drawn coaches and carriages remained a common form of transportation. The sailboats at the left look ready for a fun day on the river and bay.

This building was purchased in 1907 by John and Lou Viereck, who operated Viereck's Ice Cream Parlor. People from Toms River and other surrounding towns came to enjoy delicious homemade treats. Folks living on the other side of the river came over by boat to patronize Viereck's. Located just a half block up the hill from the bathing beach on Central Avenue, it was a popular meeting place.

The Episcopal church in Island Heights was built in the late 1880s. After serving many years in that capacity, it was purchased by the Odd Fellows and used as their meetinghouse. It now houses the Island Heights Studio of Art. It is located on the northeast corner of Central and Ocean Avenues, and is just one block up the hill from the Toms River.

St. Gertrude's Catholic Church, a branch of St. Joseph's in Toms River, was built in the late 1800s and is still used for services and weddings. There is no heat in the building, so it is used only during warm months. It is located on the northwest corner of Central and Ocean Avenues, directly across the street from the Island Heights Studio of Art.

As the town became populated with more year-round residents, a permanent church building seemed necessary, so in 1882 land was donated by members of the congregation and the Methodist Episcopal Church was built. The cornerstone of this building was laid on August 29, 1882, at the corner of Van Sant and Simpson Avenues. The site is now a parking lot for the Methodist church.

In 1925, the old building was sold and razed. Timbers from it were used to build a home on Ocean Avenue. The present Methodist church and fellowship hall stand on the corner of Ocean and Simpson Avenues. The building is an exact copy of a church seen in New England by two members of the Island Heights Methodist Church. They offered to raise the money for the church if the trustees would erect the building exactly as planned. The interior has unpainted arched wooden beams, and the construction resembles a small cathedral.

In the early 1920s, a pavilion was built at the Central Avenue public dock. From here residents could watch the boat races and other activities taking place on the Toms River. It is still a popular gathering place on warm summer evenings. Band concerts are often enjoyed by residents and visitors here at the pavilion.

Numerous pleasure boats of various kinds are docked at this pier at the foot of Simpson Avenue. This riverfront scene, with the large Victorian homes on the hillside, was typical during the 1920s. The two cars to the left are heading west on River Avenue.

This view from the bluff shows two private docks, the public dock, and the pavilion at the foot of Central Avenue extending into the river. The farthest bridge with the open span is the Pennsylvania Railroad bridge that carried train passengers back and forth between Pine Beach and Island Heights. As automobiles became more numerous, rail service was no longer needed. Service was discontinued in 1931, and the bridge was dismantled in 1934.

The river offered opportunities for recreation year-round: when it was frozen, the brave ventured out with their automobiles to drive across to Pine Beach. A few embarrassed souls occasionally discovered that the ice was not strong enough to support the weight of their cars.

As Island Heights became a substantial community, the need for increased public services became apparent; this resulted in the building of the first firehouse at the corner of Van Sant and Simpson Avenues. It is now the home of the Ocean County String Band.

The Island Heights Yacht Club (on the left), followed by the Edgewater Hotel and then the Central Avenue pavilion, were prominent structures on the waterfront. The yacht club is still a very active organization both in town and in the Barnegat Bay Yacht Racing Association. The members sponsor sailing courses for children and adults of all ages from Island Heights as well as surrounding communities. The high bluff just to the right of the pavilion was the site of the camp meeting grounds; it is said to be the highest point on the New Jersey coast south of Atlantic Highlands.

Four

SOUTH TOMS RIVER

William Giberson owned a sawmill located west of Main Street and along the river. After the mill burned, he built another mill on the hill south of Shreve Pond, on the opposite side of Main Street. He built this row of homes in the late 1880s for his employees and their families. The houses were on a road perpendicular to South Main Street, and they extended to the creek. A northeast storm with a lot of rain, along with the breaking of a dam in Pine Lake Park, raised the tide very high and the flooding shown here was the result.

The Toms River is flanked by the towns of Toms River and South Toms River. The A.B. Newbury Lumber Company (bordering the creek in the lower left), the United Feed Company, the Poultrymen's Service Corporation, and freight cars of the Jersey Central Railroad are clustered along both sides of South Main Street and Flint Road. Boats edge Huddy Park, Kirk's Boat Works, the Toms River Yacht Club, and Hainer Cove. The Riverview Hotel and Point (in Toms River) are visible at the upper right.

The *Vivienne* is shown here docked at Kirk's Boat Works. Boats are also tied up along the south shore of the river. The Jersey Central Railroad station is visible to the right. The tanks on the dock have a sign which reads "Gasolene 74."

This view is of the intersection of South Main Street and Route 9/4. The new (1930s) highway went along the river toward Beachwood instead of following Flint Boulevard, which ran south of the Jersey Central tracks. The Poultrymen's Service Corporation is on the right. Officers in 1953–54 were: David A. Veeder, president; Reginald V. Page, vice-president; and Max Leet, secretary-treasurer. The Mormon church, 30-by-40 feet, was built on this land, which belonged to Anthony Ivins, in the 1840s. In 1852 many Mormons migrated to Salt Lake City, and the church closed about 1870.

South Toms River is shown here in a photograph taken from Huddy Park. The largest building to the right of center is the United Feed Company, which was begun in 1919 by Samuel Kaufman and Herman J. (Jerry) Samuelson after they purchased the Murphy Feed business. The Kaufmans and Samuelsons had migrated from Brooklyn to Ocean County where they became chicken farmers. The growth of poultry farming after World War II increased the demand for feed, which was met by United Feed with branch stores in Lakewood, Point Pleasant, Freehold, and Jamesburg. The South Toms River building burned in the 1960s.

The William T. Giberson sawmill, shown here *c.* 1890, was in operation from the late 1880s to the early 1900s. Mr. Giberson bought cedar swamps, cut them off, and sawed lumber and shingles. He also made the old-fashioned two-part cranberry crates which were once used exclusively in New Jersey. In addition to this mill, he also had businesses in Tuckerton and West Creek.

Cranberry bogs and ponds formed ideal ice-skating rinks. Teachers from Toms River are shown here enjoying the wintry weather in January 1940. The skaters are, from left to right: Joan Bader, Ruth Neutzling, Dorothy Cook, Marie Hausherr, Bessie McLean, and Frank Halpin.

William T. Giberson (1858–1932) spent most of his life at this house on South Main Street. He married Althea Imlay on December 21, 1887. Their children (probably the three girls shown here at the left near the fence) were Mrs. Laura Morey, Mrs. Bernice Tilton, and Miss Anna Geneva Giberson. In his later years, William spent winters in Florida, where he bought land and built houses just as he had done in the Toms River area. He had homes in both Tampa and Miami. Althea died in 1922.

William T. Giberson and his sister, Annie Corson, were from Baltimore originally.

Henry Wills (holding the plow handles) and George Bogert (the young man in the big hat) are marking or plowing a line for cutting ice on Shreve's Pond, c. 1907. The workers wore metal-spiked grippers called "creepers" for traction on the ice. After the ice was cut, it was hauled by wagon to an ice house to preserve it. Shreve's Pond, part of Jake's Branch of the Toms River, was probably named for Kezia Shreve, the grandmother of Anthony Ivins (who owned the pond).

Men used long ice saws to cut through the thick layer of ice on Shreve's Pond. Long poles were then used to maneuver the chunks of ice so they could be loaded on the waiting wagons visible among the trees. In the warmer months of the year, the ice was sold to residents all along the river and across the bay at Seaside Heights, Seaside Park, and Island Beach.

Caleb Falkinburg's grist mill on Jake's Branch dates from the mid-1800s. Following the sale of the mill to John C. Lake in the 1880s, it was converted to a talcum powder mill. Hard talc stone was brought in by rail from southern states and ground into talcum powder. A famous member of the Lake family was Simon Lake, who invented, built, and tested a submarine in Toms River in 1894. The *Argonaut Junior* became the first ocean-going submarine when it traveled above and below the surface from Norfolk, Virginia, to New York in 1898.

These men are loading ice from the pond by the Falkinburg Mill.

There were numerous cranberry bogs in South Toms River, and the Jeffrey bogs were among the largest. Others were south of Flint Boulevard and south of the Pennsylvania and Long Branch railroad tracks on Jake's Branch. Harvesting cranberries was often undertaken by the whole family. Methods have changed from picking by hand in a dry bog, through the use of scoops, to using machinery in flooded bogs. New Jersey has been in the top three cranberry-producing states since the mid-1800s.

This waterfront scene was photographed from the highway between Toms River and Beachwood. The area west of the Esso station is a public park called Mathis Plaza. Across the river are the water towers and church spires of Toms River.

Trains departing from 23rd Avenue and Liberty Street in New York City paved the way for residents of New York and the north Jersey metropolitan area to come to Ocean County. Passenger service was discontinued in 1952 but freight continued to be delivered until the 1980s. This train is arriving from Lakehurst at the station of the Central Railroad of New Jersey. The station burned on March 17, 1976, and what remained was razed. It was located across the river from Huddy Park, east of South Main Street, near its intersection with Flint Boulevard. The A.B. Newbury Lumber Company can be seen on the left.

Grace Richtmeyer and Roy Tilton are shown here at their golden wedding anniversary. Their home, where they raised four children, was at the southwest corner of Dover Road and Tilton Avenue, though their property at one time had extended to Jake's Branch. Mr. Tilton was an officer of the First National Bank, while Grace served on the Toms River Schools Board of Education, held local and state offices in the Order of the Eastern Star, and was one of the first women elected to be an elder and trustee of the Presbyterian Church of Toms River.

The A.B. Newbury lumber and coal business was located on the former site of the Mormon church—on the Toms River, on the west side of South Main Street near the Central Railroad depot, just where the Central Railroad bridge crossed the river. The small lumber business was started about 1865, and it was purchased around 1880 by William Aumack. He later sold it to Amos Birdsall Newbury, who named it the A.B. Newbury Company. In 1900, the company operated with four employees and two teams of horses.

From modest beginnings, the A.B. Newbury Company expanded its facilities and was considered to have the most complete and up-to-date building supply display room anywhere in this part of New Jersey. After Captain Newbury died in 1906, Mr. Jesse P. Evernham took over the business as manager and continued until his death on May 27, 1953. By 1915, the business employed forty-seven workers and sixteen teams of horses, which were later replaced with a large fleet of trucks for deliveries. The Seaport Market occupies the premises today.

The Toms River station of the Pennsylvania Railroad was located at the end of South Main Street. In 1881, the railroad was called the Philadelphia and Long Branch Railroad. In that same year, John Walton was awarded the contract to build a "two-story frame building, Swiss cottage style, slate roof, and projecting eaves." The first floor contained the 16-by-18-foot passenger room, and a living room and kitchen for the use of the agent's family. The second floor contained two commodious bedrooms with spacious closets.

This train from Philadelphia is on its way across Barnegat Bay via the bridge to Seaside Park and up along the shore of the Atlantic Ocean. When the bridge burned in 1946, passengers disembarked at South Toms River and were transported to Seaside Park via the bus seen in the background. The bus was operated by Pillion and Shibla. One station agent was Allen W. Sever, who held the position from 1907 until his death on April 23, 1924. When the tracks were removed to make way for the Route 9 connection with the Garden State Parkway, the building was moved to Beachwood, about a half mile east, and is currently used as a private home.

Birdville, which still stands, has a most interesting history. Albert P. Greim built a factory here in 1915 to manufacture bird boxes. To study bird habits he lived in a tree house at first. When he finally built his home, he installed a small chapel and a $10,000 pipe organ. Moravian tiles, made by Henry Chapman Mercer of Doylestown, Pennsylvania, were set into the concrete walls around Birdville and in the case around the organ. Mr. Greim's birdhouse business was most successful and became known worldwide. Birdville was used for church services, weddings, and borough council meetings. Mr. Greim died in 1933.

Faunce's Boat Works, shown here c. 1905, was located on Cedar Point on the south side of the river, a bit downriver from Kirk's Boat Works and Riverview Point. Faunce provided repair and maintenance service to smaller boats along the river. A catboat waiting to be repaired sits on the dry dock railway. Father George and two sons, George and Harry, owned the business in the early 1900s. Harry, who resided on Locust Street, still operated a boat business in the 1940s.

Five

BEACHWOOD

The Polyhue Yacht Club, a "real" yacht club, was planned for Beachwood in 1920. At first, there had been a club to which all lot owners belonged without having to pay dues. The new club was to consist only of those interested in boating. A fleet of eight 15-foot sneakboxes was ordered from J. Howard Perrine, a noted shipbuilder of Barnegat. The first boats were delivered in time for the Memorial Day races in 1921. In keeping with the club's name, each sail was a different color. Club members decided to join the Barnegat Bay Yacht Racing Association in 1921.

Indian Joe was Beachwood's sole resident at one time. He returned in 1923 to set up his wigwam just below the little bridge over Jake's Branch on the way to Toms River.

In the late 1800s, charcoal was loaded onto sailing vessels in the area that includes Beachwood's bathing beach and the banks just to the east along Windy Cove. The charcoal was made about 10 miles inland in Manchester Township and brought by donkey-drawn cars on tracks to the dock in Windy Cove. After the charcoal trade ceased, the pilings that remained led to calling this location "The Spiles." Bits of charcoal can still be unearthed on the beach.

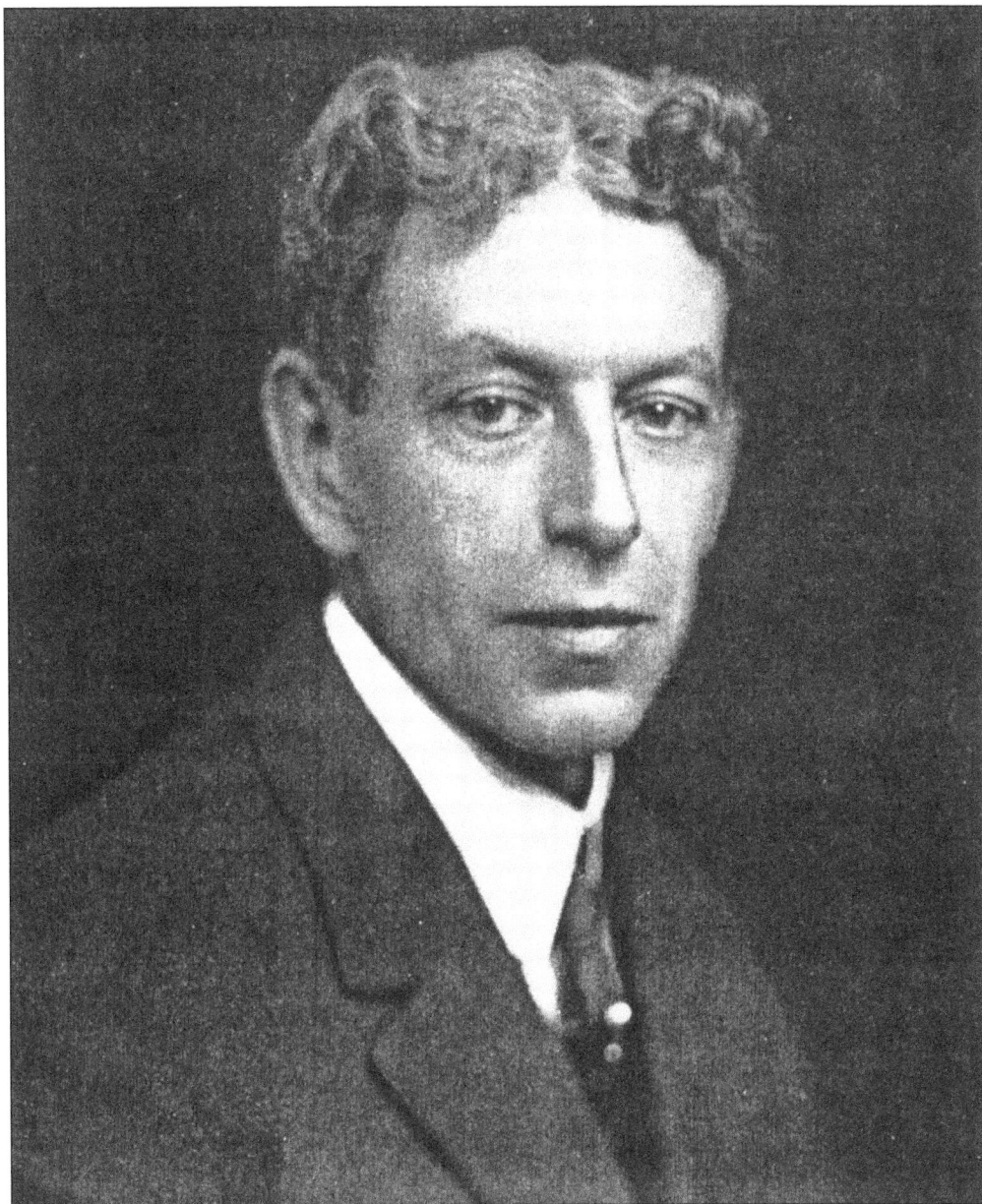

Bertram C. Mayo founded Beachwood. He was born in Boston in 1865, became a clothing salesman, and then entered the field of journalism. To encourage newspaper sales, he promoted, through the sale of lots with a subscription, the development of communities in Caseredo, California; Lakewood, Michigan; and Beachwood and Browns Mills in New Jersey. Mr. Mayo died at the age of fifty-five, just six short years after Beachwood was started, but he had already become its greatest benefactor. He donated the clubhouse and promenade, the lodge and auditorium, the railroad station and seven surrounding lots, and the riverfront property on which the public buildings were located. A large tract between the clubhouse and Harpoon Street was made available to the borough at the original cost of the lots. This is today's Mayo Park, which includes ball fields, a picnic area, a playground, and a park along the top of the bluffs.

The Jersey Central Railroad began dropping off passengers in Beachwood by 1915. A year later the Pennsylvania Railroad erected a loading platform and began making stops in Beachwood. However, both railroad companies refused to put up buildings of their own. Mr. Mayo, undaunted by this lack of cooperation, put up his own station (shown here), which was later acquired by the borough along with seven surrounding lots.

A signal station and switch were essential at Beachwood where the Jersey Central and Pennsylvania tracks crossed in Ocean County. The trains originated in Jersey City and Camden, respectively. Today, Route 9, between Exit 80 of the Garden State Parkway and Atlantic City Boulevard in Beachwood, follows the path of the Pennsylvania Railroad.

This was the Central
Railroad of New Jersey's
schedule of service
between New York
and Beachwood for
June 29–September 28,
1924. The trip one way
took between three and
three-and-a-half hours.
The route included stops at
Jackson Avenue, Newark,
Elizabeth, and Red Bank.

CENTRAL RAILROAD OF NEW JERSEY

TRAIN SERVICE BETWEEN NEW YORK AND BEACHWOOD

Summer Time Table only. It went into effect June 29, 1924, and will continue in effect until September 28th.

Standard Time. Daylight Saving Time is one hour later		**WEEKDAYS**						**SUNDAY**
			Sat. Only	Except Sat.	Sat. Only			
Lv. New York, W. 23rd St......	A.M.	A.M. 7.45	A.M. 11.45	A.M. 11.30	P.M.	P.M. 3.45		A.M. 6.47
Lv. New York, Liberty St.......	2.30	8.00	12.00	11.45	12.30	4.05		7.10
Lv. Jackson Avenue		8.18	11.40	11.40	12.21	3.37		7.29
Lv. Newark........		8.05	11.54	11.54	12.35	3.25		7.22
Lv. Elizabeth......	3.05	8.14	12.06	11.58	12.39	3.22		7.05
Lv. Red Bank......	5.40	9.13	1.07	1.24	1.59	5.14		8.52
Ar. Beachwood.....	7.27	10.17	1.57	2.57	3.32	6.29		10.01
	A.M.	A.M.	P.M.	P.M.	P.M.	P.M.		A.M.

	WEEKDAYS				**SUNDAY**
	A.M.	A.M.	P.M.	P.M.	P.M.
Lv. Beachwood.................	5.36	9.03	2.13	5.01	6.18
Ar. Red Bank.................	6.53	10.12	3.18	6.43	7.32
Ar. Elizabeth.................	8.03	11.05	4.12	8.07	8.32
Ar. Newark...................	8.25	11.16	4.18	8.23	8.42
Ar. Jackson Avenue...........	8.38	11.08	4.31	8.28	8.41
Ar. New York, Liberty St.......	8.20	11.28	4.25	8.25	9.00
Ar. New York, W. 23rd St.......	8.42	11.40	4.37	8.37	9.12
	A.M.	A.M.	P.M.	P.M.	P.M.

The Lodge, including a clubhouse and dining room, was built by Mr. Mayo on the bluff above the bathing beach. In 1917 he offered "Beachwood Point" (which had been reserved for him and which was the location of the Lodge) plus 209 choice lots on both sides of Bayside Avenue to the borough at the original purchase price of $19.60 each. The borough accepted Mr. Mayo's offer and set the lots aside as a park—Mayo Park.

THE LIFE AT THE PIER, BEACHWOOD, N. J.

These children participating in sack races have a large audience. The bathing beach, with its pier, diving board, and high dive tower, has always been a very popular spot. On the Fourth of July, land and swimming races are held, and a fireworks display at night attracts viewers from many committees, hundreds of whom come by boat. Today Beachwood is the only town along the river which continues its fireworks display.

In front of the Polyhue Yacht Club two boardwalks merge, one coming down from Spring Street and Bayside Avenue and the other coming from the west end of the Beachwood waterfront. Spring Street's name came from the delightful little spring near the water's edge where early residents filled their water jugs. It still oozes water today.

98

This idyllic scene represents all that Bertram C. Mayo hoped for as he planned the development of communities. He wanted to bring recreation homes within the means of the mass of people. His criteria called for a spot accessible to a large population center, with a healthy environment, and possessing natural beauty. Beachwood filled the bill.

CAT RIG
FOR BAY AND
RIVER USE
$235.

The above shows the kind of boat which the **Polyhue Yacht Club of Beachwood** uses exclusively in racing events. The sails used are of different colors, making a beautiful sight.

200 of these famous boats have also been adopted by various other Yacht Clubs for One Design Class racing and have proved wonderfully fast and satisfactory.

Built of selected Jersey cedar and white oak. Copper nails riveted. Hulls painted inside and out.

Wearing strips, waist and cock-pit coaming are finished bright with best grade of SPAR VARNISH.

All SPARS are of SPRUCE, finished bright. Only the best grade MANILLA used in rigging. Weight complete about 400 pounds.

J. H. PERRINE, Designer and Builder

BARNEGAT   NEW JERSEY
ESTABLISHED 1900

The sneakbox was a favorite racing boat on Toms River. This advertisement by J.H. Perrine, a leading designer and builder, shows a cat-rigged boat for use on the bay or the river. It was made of selected Jersey cedar and white oak with copper nails. The spars were made of spruce and the best grade manila was used in the rigging. The Perrine sneakbox weighed about 400 pounds and cost $235.

The Beachwood Rod and Gun Club was organized in 1920. Plans to build a log cabin went awry when the supply of logs was destroyed by fire. Instead, they erected a concrete block clubhouse at the west end of Chestnut Street near Jakes Branch of the Toms River. Members cleared the ground and built a roadway to the creek. A beefsteak and 'possum supper was held to raise money. Pictured here is Hattie Widmaier, whose family owned a bakery in Brooklyn. She came to the "wilds" of Beachwood, learned to handle a rifle, and married a local Toms River boy named Lee Campbell.

Although Beachwood began as a summer resort and most cottages were unheated, a few people, like George S. Thain, built substantial winterized houses. Here Estelle Thain, one of six children, enjoys the ice during a winter vacation. Two sisters, Ellathea Thain and Georgianna Tracy, still live in the Toms River area. J.W. Finley of Finley Fuel and Mrs. Thomas Kelaher (Carol) are great-grandchildren of George S. and Emma Thain.

The Talmage bungalow was located on Barnegat Boulevard between Spring and Lookout Streets. Mr. Talmage of Brooklyn tried his hand at art, studied law, and finally entered the business world for over fifty years. He was chairman of Beachwood's first borough council and treasurer of both the Property Owners' Association and the yacht club. Mrs. Talmage was president of the Women's Club for two years.

Bungalows were the most popular type of house built in Beachwood. They were usually only one story and had one or more screened-in porches. Most were built for summer use only and were without heat or plumbing. A well and pump supplied water. Not until after World War II were most of the homes made into year-round residences. This one, built in 1915 on Ship Avenue, with its trellis in front and grape arbor in back, belonged to William and Frieda Widmaier of Brooklyn.

MRS. CLINTON H. HOARD
Second President, Woman's Club

MRS. GEORGE D. SIFFERT
President, Woman's Club, 1921-1924

The Beachwood Women's Club was organized in 1916 by women with the foresight to realize the importance of social interaction in community development. Social programs included a weekly children's dance, afternoon teas, concerts, moonlight sails, cake sales, and a community dance on Saturday evenings. These were some of the area's leading women: Mrs. Clinton H. Hoard, Mrs. William H. Talmage, Mrs. George D. Siffert, and Mrs. Edwin D. Collins.

Mrs. Wanda E. Lohr is credited with urging the development of some system of fire protection. Through her efforts and the cooperation of various organizations and borough officials, a grand fair was held in 1921 under the auspices of the Property Owners' Association. Almost $2,000 was raised, enough to purchase a handsome four-wheel chemical fire engine at the cost of $1,645.99. The Beachwood Volunteer Company #1 firehouse and borough hall was dedicated on July 4, 1923. It has been the home of the fire company ever since. New borough offices were erected in 1955 on Pinewald Road.

102

CHAS. H. HARING

WM. TALMAGE

B. J. FORSYTHE

JOS. H. SENIOR
Mayor

M. L. STIMSON

ALBERT WILLIAMS

GEO. D. SUYDAM

Mayor Joseph H. Senior and the borough council organized for business in January 1918. George D. Suydam was elected president. The mayor appointed Max Blasberg as clerk, Frank J. Turner as marshall, William Howard Jeffrey as borough attorney, and John J. Kearin as collector. A budget of $12,000, to be raised by taxes, was adopted for the year. Mr. Turner was the only policeman in the community for many years.

Frank E. McCraigh's advertisement in the *Beachwood Borough Directory and Who's Who* (1924), portrayed him as the first to open a real estate business and store in Beachwood. The store, which carried a full line of delicatessen delicacies, candies, and cigars, was located on the east side of Beachwood Boulevard near the Jersey Central Railroad station. Mr. McCraigh was born in Boston, had a grocery business in Jersey City, and was a Beachwood pioneer.

103

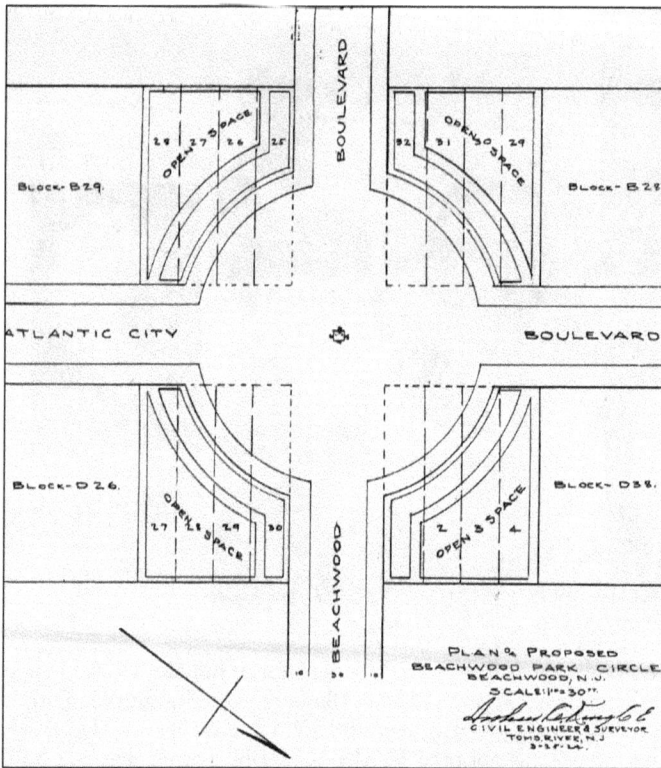

An ordinance adopted on May 3, 1924, provided for the widening of Beachwood Boulevard at its intersection with Atlantic City Boulevard, and the laying out of an open space to be known as Beachwood Park Circle (shown here). In 1995 that open space still exists on the north side of Atlantic City Boulevard (now Route 166). The area on the south side is occupied by stores.

The Beachwood Post Office was opened for business in the railroad station building on March 1, 1921, with William B. Brown having been appointed postmaster. Up to that time, year-round residents (twenty families in 1921) picked up their mail at the clubhouse in Toms River, or put up rural delivery boxes. Edmund A. Smith, appointed postmaster in 1918, used facilities like the W.T. Burnett store and J.G. Browning's little office building for an office until 1921. In 1957 the U.S. Post Office moved into its own building on Locker Street.

Six

PINE BEACH

Among this array of bathers at the Henley Avenue pier in 1915 are members of the Wheeler, Giblin, Hottenstein, Buckholtz, Kurtz, Dittman, Fager, Bauer, Doughty, Walsh, Shuster, Mulrennan, and Sheeran families. In summer the way to spend day after day was at the beach and in the water. Bathing suits were one-piece or two-piece, men's suits still included tops, many women wore caps of some kind, and women's suits were knee-length or longer. (Courtesy of Louise Hottenstein.)

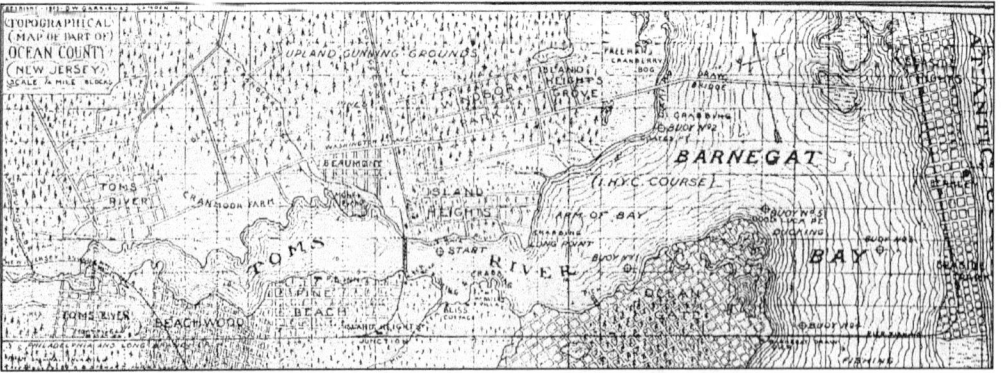

The "Bays and Hills Map of Old Barnegat" was circulated a few years before 1920 by merchants of Toms River. It shows that the area around and in the Toms River Estuary was great for hunting, fishing, and crabbing. Berkeley separated from Dover Township in 1875. In the early 1900s three boroughs were created from Berkeley Township on the south bank of the river, but Berkeley retained a small tract between Pine Beach and Ocean Gate which included Mill Creek.

Where the Sea and Pines Meet

~ Pine Beach Inn ~
Pine Beach, N. J.

Situated on Barnegat Bay. In the midst of the Pines, midway between Long Branch and Atlantic City, and right close to Beachwood. Offers the Vacationist an ideal vacation. Home cooking. Light, cheerful rooms with or without bath, single or ensuite. Dancing, Boating, Bathing, Fishing. Saddle horses for hire.

Special attention to Tourists

Write for Rates

ALBERT SCHWEIGART
Pine Beach, N. J.

'Phone 239

Another dream of Robert Horter, the developer of Pine Beach, was realized with the construction of the Pine Beach Inn. With the death in 1915 of George Kelly, financier and president of the Pine Beach Improvement Company, the inn closed. It stood idle until it was purchased by Albert Schweigart in 1922 for less than $11,000 (the original cost in 1910 was reputed to be $150,000). Despite ads such as this the inn did not do well; therefore, in 1933, the property was sold to the Admiral Farragut Academy.

106

Looking westward along the waterfront at the Henley Avenue pier, the Yacht Club and the Pine Beach Inn can be seen. The boat at the dock is probably one of the boats that carried passengers up and down the river.

The Pine Beach Inn, which opened in 1910, had a beautiful setting and view of the Toms River. It faced the bluffs of Money Island across the river. On the opposite shore downriver lay the Island Heights Camp Meeting Association's property. State law prohibited the sale of liquor within 1 mile of any camp meeting property. Fortunately, the west end of the inn, to the right in this photograph, was 1 mile, 21 feet, and 8 inches from the camp meeting property, so the hotel grill could be placed there and a liquor license granted. After the property was sold to Admiral Farragut, it was used for offices, a dining room for the cadets, and dormitory rooms. Now, in 1995, the Admiral Farragut Academy has closed its doors and the fate of this building is undecided.

For those traveling between the Philadelphia-Camden area and Island Heights, the Island Heights Junction at Pine Beach was a familiar sight. The main track of the Philadelphia and Long Branch Railroad went through Pine Beach to Barnegat Pier and across Barnegat Bay. A spur branched off toward the river and Island Heights on the opposite bank. This station was located near the river at the foot of what is now Station Avenue. After train service to Island Heights ended, the station was moved to a lot at the east end of Riverside Drive and is privately owned today.

The trestle from Pine Beach to Island Heights was constructed in 1883 by the Philadelphia and Long Branch Railroad to provide passenger service to Island Heights, which can be seen here across the river. The bridge was a manually-operated swing bridge. Service was discontinued in 1924 and the trestle was removed in 1934. The railroad company offered to sell it to the county as an automobile bridge but the offer was declined.

The beautiful Pine Beach Inn attracted many visitors.

The parallel tracks through Pine Beach allowed passengers going to Island Heights to alight at the Pine Beach station and board the smaller dummy train for the short trip to their destination. A huge Y permitted trains to approach the trestle from one arm of the Y and return to the main track on the other arm, if desired. (Courtesy of Louise Hottenstein.)

The first house built in Pine Beach still stands today at 402 Henley Avenue. It was erected by Roy Hutchinson in 1909 for the Reverend August Pohlman. Roy Hutchinson was one of the first residents and a longtime builder in Pine Beach. Roy and his brother Howard lived in a tent through the summer of 1909 while they built the first of several hundred homes. They then started work on their own houses. Both became leading citizens of the community.

This 1970s view is of the building at 816 Linden Avenue that served as Henry Clayton's store in 1909 and as the first post office in 1910. Mr. Clayton was the first postmaster and served as a councilman from 1928 to 1930.

110

The Henley Avenue pier was constructed in the spring of 1909 for area residents and so that the passenger boats *Ariella* and *Dorianna*, operated by Captain Ira Lambert between Toms River and Seaside Heights, could make regular stops. The fare was 15¢ to Toms River and 20¢ to Seaside. It is likely that residents made regular trips to Toms River for food and other necessities and traveled to Seaside for a day at the ocean.

These houses were located along Riverside Drive, east of Henley Avenue. The railroad station was between Henley and Cedar Avenues, where Pennsylvania Avenue is today. The yacht club was a short distance to the west along Riverside Drive. This area must have been considered a prime location.

A sneakbox was photographed at the Buhler Mansion pier, c. 1905. In 1877 George Burnett, a New York hatter, is believed to have built a fourteen-room house with a fireplace in every room and pipes for gas lights. The estate was acquired in 1903 by William Buhler, a New York financier who committed suicide in 1910. It passed through several other hands before becoming the home of Admiral Robison, a superintendent of the Admiral Farragut Academy, in 1939. The greatly-modified original mansion still stands screened by houses recently built along the edge of the property. It was bounded at one time by Motor Road and Riverside, Buhler, Avon, and Radnor Avenues.

The Pine Beach Yacht Club came into existence in 1916 with William Wilson as its first commodore. Joseph Woods, the president of the Pine Beach Improvement Company, donated land, and the one-story clubhouse was completed in the spring of 1916 at a cost of $1,500. The Ladies Auxiliary planned both social activities and fund-raising events to raise the clubhouse, and a new first floor added in 1921. One of the very faithful members who made this club such a success was Mrs. John (Carrie) Mergenthaler, who completed fifty-two years of membership in 1975. (Courtesy of Louise Hottenstein.)

These umbrellas at the dock in front of the Buhler house raise several questions. Was it raining or was it just a very hot sunny day? Were they waiting for a boat or had they simply come to the river's edge to enjoy the view? Who are they? Visitors of the Buhlers? The dock was directly across the river from the east end of Cranmoor Manor. Downriver to the right Money Island's bluffs and the community of Island Heights could be seen.

The Admiral Farragut Academy was first opened in September 1933 and initially consisted of 4 acres of land and fifty-six students. The Academy has a proud history of quality education. Many of its graduates entered the service academies and served well in our nation's conflicts. Admiral Alan B. Shepard, our country's first astronaut, is a graduate of the Class of 1941 and the Academy's most famous alumnus. After sixty-one years as a good neighbor and part of the greater Toms River and Pine Beach communities, the Academy closed in 1994. At that time, it had increased its enrollment to two hundred and fifty students, and its campus consisted of 28 acres. The cadets and their sports, parades, band, and dances are missed.

The Pine Villa, a boarding house located at 519 New Jersey Avenue, was owned by the Bordt family. A pier was built at New Jersey Avenue in 1922.

The Pine Beach Yacht Club can be seen here in this view eastward along Riverside Avenue. The end of World War II and the opening of the Garden State Parkway increased population in these river communities and made more money available for recreation. The interest in sailing has increased since then and the club has once again become an active part of the yachting scene on both the river and the bay. At one time the Pine Beach Yacht Club had the largest fleet of snipes in New Jersey.

This photograph of the water tower serves as a symbol of the early days of Pine Beach, when few houses had indoor plumbing, roads were unpaved, and mosquitoes were abundant. When Pine Beach became a borough in 1925 it was 3/4 square miles, and had about 120 houses, 2 stores, Winterling's gas station (now the Lamp Post Inn), the Pine Beach Inn, a chapel, the yacht club, and fifty year-round residents. (Courtesy of Louise Hottenstein.)

Women and children often made up the population from Monday through Friday in the summer months, with men being present only on weekends. (Courtesy of Louise Hottenstein.)

The "Cement House" was built in 1909 for Dr. Earle C. Rice at 709 Riverside Drive. The tax a year later was $15.04. Cement, instead of the usual wood, was used to build this home because of Dr. Rice's fear of forest fires. Alan Lake Rice, Dr. Rice's son, described Riverside Drive as a grand name: "The Drive wasn't cut through until the second year and it ran only from Henley Avenue, past the Rice home, to 'the swamp' now the Admiral Farragut football field, where Midland Avenue now intersects." (Courtesy of Louise Hottenstein.)

Rocking chairs were essential features of any good porch. Much time was spent on the screened-in porches. Often the house itself was a small structure with small rooms, but the porches, which often wrapped around a corner, were ample enough to allow for games, hammocks, gatherings, and swings. (Courtesy of Louise Hottenstein.)

116

Seven

OCEAN GATE

These three houses along the boardwalk in Ocean Gate exemplify the architectural changes that occurred as Ocean Gate developed. At first there were small summer bungalows with screened-in porches (at the left). The middle house is a bit larger, and the one on the right includes two full stories and seems to have been enlarged considerably by the addition to the front. (Courtesy of Ocean Gate Historical Society.)

The railroad was Ocean Gate's lifeline. Ice cut during the winter near Toms River came via the train in the summer. Local merchants met the train to pick up their supplies. Kiesel's Dairy sent milk. The mail arrived twice a day and was carted to Page's grocery store, where the post office was located. The station has been located at three different sites: on Bayview Avenue (1909–1952), on a site behind the Borough Hall (1952–1990), and on the corner of Asbury and Cape May Avenue (1990–present). It has been converted into a museum by the Ocean Gate Historical Society. (Courtesy of the Ocean Gate Historical Society.)

Floyd W. Mease, in *Memories of Bygone Days*, states that Charles Guttentag and the Great Eastern Building Corporation of which he was president "purchased farmland, advertised in Philadelphia newspapers, took prospects on a free train ride to Ocean Gate, fed them at the Grant farmhouse and sold them lots on the installment plan." As in other small communities along the Toms River, the train was the key factor in Ocean Gate's development. (Courtesy of the Ocean Gate Historical Society.)

118

Dinners and light snacks were served at Kiesel's Restaurant, and customers could enjoy rocking chairs on the porch. Ray Kiesel's dairy on Ocean Gate Avenue served customers from Seaside Heights and Seaside Park to Barnegat. Milk was obtained from local farmers or brought in by train. (Courtesy of the Ocean Gate Historical Society.)

About 1920 the town council began plans to build an 8-foot-wide boardwalk. Today 1 mile of that boardwalk still exists, making it the longest wooden walkway in any of the river communities. In 1919, the purchase of sixty poles and sixty Dietz kerosene lamps was authorized. One of these lamps is visible in this photograph. Jacob Ringelstein was appointed lamplighter and paid $40 a month. (Courtesy of the Ocean Gate Historical Society.)

Crowds of tourists are shown here at the Barnegat Pier station. A day's trip could be made from Philadelphia to the shore and many city-dwellers took advantage of the opportunity. The well-dressed passengers here look quite different from those bound for the beaches today. (Courtesy of the Ocean Gate Historical Society.)

The first automobile bridge connecting Toms River and the beach strip from Bay Head to Island Beach can be seen here in the background. E-scows racing across the Wanamaker course on Barnegat Bay remain a familiar summer sight.

The Barnegat Pier station was built out over the bay along the railroad trestle. For some passengers the pier was their destination, and they spent the day fishing and enjoying the invigorating sea breezes that swept across the bay. In David Anderson's funeral records, for a period in the early 1900s, individuals that died at Barnegat Pier had that listed as their place of death, rather than the name of the larger community.

Barnegat Pier seems to have been the name given not only to the pier but also to the little community that developed along the bay in that part of Berkeley Township. Today, the Water's Edge Restaurant stands on the site of the three houses to the left of the signal pole in this photograph. The signal controlled trains traveling east and west. Only a few pilings of the trestle remain.

The beach at Ocean Gate has always been a popular recreation spot. (Courtesy of the Ocean Gate Historical Society.)

Piers extending into the river from the bathing beach have been enjoyed by swimmers, crabbers, and sightseers for years. Two, in particular, suffered from the weather during World War II. The Wildwood Avenue pier was sheared off its pilings at the water line when a strong northwest wind blew ice down the river and against the pier. A few years later, the Anglesea pier simply floated away when strong southeast winds created tides of 5 to 10 feet above normal. (Courtesy of the Ocean Gate Historical Society.)

OCEAN GATE
THE RESORT SWEPT BY THE BREEZES OF OCEAN, BAY AND RIVER

COMFORT STATION AT OCEAN GATE

ONE OF THE SLIDES AT OCEAN GATE

WATCHING THE WATER SPORTS FROM ONE OF THE PIERS OCEAN GATE

One of the biggest attractions for children of all sizes and ages at Ocean Gate was the presence of two very high slides. This is the long slide at Ocean Gate. When sliders reached the bottom they were dumped into the river. (Courtesy of the Ocean Gate Historical Society.)

The Ocean Gate Yacht Club, organized in 1909, was one of the original clubs that formed the Barnegat Bay Yacht Club Association. It is situated at the mouth of Toms River where it widens and flows into the waters of Barnegat Bay. Throughout the club's history it has been an active sailing and social center of the community. This photograph, taken in 1922, shows the new porch. Another renovation was completed in 1995. (Courtesy of the Ocean Gate Historical Society.)

Pupils first attended "school" at the Grant farmhouse. The Ocean Gate schoolhouse (shown here) was erected in 1914 as School #4 in Berkeley Township. After Ocean Gate became an independent borough, the building continued to be used as the town's one-room school until 1941, when a larger school was constructed. Today, this building houses Ocean Gate's kindergarten classes. Of the seventy-six one-room schoolhouses that once existed in Ocean County, this is the only one still used as a school.

Narragansett Avenue, where the boardwalk ends, is the easternmost street in Ocean Gate. Beyond it, marshes and meadowlands extend south for miles, forming a border for Barnegat Bay.

Ocean Gate Volunteer Fire Company #1 was organized in 1913, and a firehouse was built on land donated by the Great Eastern Building Corporation at Wildwood and Long Beach Avenues. A fire ring, which still remains outside the firehouse, was used to sound the alarm. The first piece of apparatus was a hand-drawn soda and acid chemical cart which was later supplemented by a Ford Model T chemical truck. Buildings already on fire could not usually be saved; the fire company's goal was to prevent fires from spreading to surrounding buildings.

Small boats of all kinds dot the beach and shoreline. Summer residents enjoy fishing and crabbing, as well as just taking to the water for pleasure.

Horses and wagons make their way along sandy Anglesea Avenue to deliver departing passengers or take arriving ones to their destinations, c. 1915. Note the train, visible to the right.

Mrs. Emily Sever Groetzinger was the daughter of Allen W. Sever, a station agent for the Pennsylvania Railroad in South Toms River. When she married Jack Groetzinger she moved to Ocean Gate. She kept the books for her husband's plumbing business, and during World War II fought local fires while serving as president of the Ocean County Women's Fire Fighting Corps, which was organized to serve while the men were at war. After the war she served in countless civic and political organizations. She is shown here with Congressman James Auchincloss and members of the Republican Party.

Crabbing has afforded more pleasure on the river and bay than any other fishing pursuit. It was often done from docks, utilizing metal traps. In this picture crabs are being caught by line from the back of a sail boat.

Shella Mick

The Ocean County Historical Society and its museum play vital roles in preserving the county's history, in hosting those who want a glimpse of the past, and in disseminating information through exhibits, programs, trips, research facilities, and publications. It all began in 1950 at the time of Ocean County's centennial celebration. A group of citizens was inspired to form a historical society to serve the entire county. Artifacts were collected and first displayed in a hallway in the courthouse. When the county condemned properties in the late 1960s, the Society purchased the Sculthorpe house on Hooper Avenue, which was built by the Taylor Irons family in 1828. Land was donated by John Manning Birdsall and the house was moved one block eastward to Hadley Avenue. There the house was set on a larger foundation to provide for two exhibit areas, the Birdsall Room in the basement and the Pauline S. Miller Room on the first floor. On June 7, 1973, the museum opened. It offered eight Victorian display rooms, two exhibit areas, and a tiny office for genealogical research. In the ensuing years many more artifacts were donated and school groups and people from around the county came to visit. By 1989 it was evident that more space was essential. In October 1990 a new building, attached by a connecting room and containing the Richard L. Strickler Research Center and the Myrtle Moore Exhibit Room, was opened. In 1995 a computer system was installed and a full-time curator was hired—indicators of the Society's growing service to the community and the dedication of its members. The Society is an independent organization but relies heavily upon the Ocean County Board of Freeholders for support and assistance with finances and staff.